The National Games and National Identity in China

The history of China's National Games reflects both the transformation of elite sport in China and wider Chinese society. This is the first book to describe the origins and development of the National Games through their dynamic relationship with Chinese politics, nationalism and identity in the modern era.

Looking specifically at the role of the National Games in China's changing social, political and economic circumstances from 1910 to 2009, this book uncovers how the National Games reflected the shifts in state-led nationalist ideologies within three historical eras: the late Qing Dynasty and Republican China (1910–1948), the early People's Republic of China (1959–1979) and the People's Republic of China in the post-1980s (1983–2009). It also examines how the National Games were reformed to serve China's Olympic Strategy in the context of globalization and commercialization from the 1980s onwards. Full of original insights into archive material, each chapter sheds new light on the social, cultural and political significance of this sporting mega-event in the shaping of modern China.

This is fascinating reading for anybody with an interest in the politics, history and culture of China.

Liu Li is a lecturer in the College of Sports and Physical Education at Anhui Normal University, China.

Fan Hong is Professor of Asian Studies at Bangor University, UK.

Routledge Focus on Sport, Culture and Society

Routledge Focus on Sport, Culture and Society showcases the latest cutting-edge research in the sociology of sport and exercise. Concise in form (20,000–50,000 words) and published quickly (within three months), the books in this series represent an important channel through which authors can disseminate their research swiftly and make an impact on current debates. We welcome submissions on any topic within the socio-cultural study of sport and exercise, including but not limited to subjects such as gender, race, sexuality, disability, politics, the media, social theory, Olympic Studies and the ethics and philosophy of sport. The series aims to be theoretically informed, empirically grounded and international in reach, and will include a diversity of methodological approaches.

Available in this series:

www.routledge.com/sport/series/RFSCS

The National Games and National Identity in China

A History

Liu Li and Fan Hong

Routledge
Taylor & Francis Group

LONDON AND NEW YORK

First published 2017 by Routledge

2 Park Square, Milton Park, Abingdon, Oxfordshire OX14 4RN
52 Vanderbilt Avenue, New York, NY 10017

Routledge is an imprint of the Taylor & Francis Group, an informa business

First issued in paperback 2019

British Library Cataloguing-in-Publication Data
A catalogue record for this book is available from the British Library

Library of Congress Cataloging-in-Publication Data
A catalog record for this book has been requested

ISBN: 978-1-138-62819-9 (hbk)
ISBN: 978-0-367-34503-7 (pbk)

Typeset in Times New Roman
by Apex CoVantage, LLC

Contents

Figures

Tables

Abbreviations

ACTFU	All China Federation of Trade Unions
ACSF	All China Sport Federation
ACWF	All China Women's Federation
AFC	Asian Football Confederation
BWS	Beijing Worker's Stadium
CBA	Chinese Basketball Association
CCNDFS	China Central Newsreel and Documentary Film Studio
CCP	China Communist Party
CCTV	China Central Television
CCYL	Chinese Communist Youth League
CFA	Chinese Football Association
CMCA	Chinese Ministry of Civil Affairs
CNAAF	China National Amateur Athletic Federation
CNP	Chinese Nationalist Party
COCADC	Chinese Olympic Committee Anti-Doping Commission
CPBS	Central People's Broadcasting Station
CPPCC	Chinese People's Political Consultative Conference
CUBA	China University Basketball Association
CWUA	Chinese Wushu Association
FECG	Far Eastern Championship Games
FIFA	Federation International of Football Association
GANEFO	Games of the New Emerging Force
GASC	General Administration of Sport of China
IOC	International Olympic Committee
IWUF	International Wushu Federation
NBSC	National Bureau of Statistic of China
NEC	Nippon Electric Company
NPC	National People's Congress
PLA	People's Liberation Army
PRC	People's Republic of China

SEZ	Special Economic Zones
SSM	State Sport Ministry
TUCNRF	Trade Unions of Chinese National Railway Federation
WADA	World Anti-Doping Agency
YMCA	Young Men's Christian Association

Preface

The *National Games of the People's Republic of China* is often known by its shortened name, the *National Games*.[1] It is sometimes translated as the *All China Games* or the *Chinese National Games*. The quadrennial National Games is fully institutionalized and represents the largest multi-sports event at national level in China. Comprising more than 10 different types of sports events, the National Games is regarded as the quintessence of elite sport in China. The Games were first held in 1910 during the late Qing Dynasty and another six times until 1948 in the Republic of China (ROC; see Appendix 1). In the PRC, under the leadership of the Chinese Communist Party (CCP), the National Games were first held in 1959. They have been held 12 times since then, with the most recent being the Games of Shenyang, Liaoning Province in October 2013 (see Appendix 2). The next National Games in China will be held in Tianjin in 2017. Most of the events of the National Games are Olympic events, except for the inclusion of some Chinese traditional indigenous Wushu (Chinese martial arts). In general, the National Games provide an opportunity for Chinese professional athletes from different regions within China to compete for excellence and enhance their skills, allowing them to better represent China on the international stage. The National Games have played an important role in China's ever-increasing involvement in international sport.

However, China's National Games are a lesser-known sports event and a relatively unexploited area of study in the West. To fill in this knowledge gap, this book depicts the origin, development and transformation of the National Games in China from historical and societal-historical perspectives. The main sources for this book are primary and secondary historical data, semi-structured interviews and participant observations.

The development of the National Games in the past decades reflects the transformation of Chinese elite sport as well as transformation of Chinese society. This book aims at developing a deeper and more nuanced understanding of dynamic interrelationship between the National Games and

Chinese national identity in the 20th and early 21st centuries. On the one hand, it attempts to describe and critically analyze the transformation process of the National Games in China. On the other hand, it interprets how the National Games reflects changing contents of Chinese nationalism as well as how the promotion of Chinese national identity can be mapped through the programmes of the National Games. Therefore, it uncovers the dynamic interrelationship between the National Games, Chinese politics and nationalism in the process of Chinese nation-building in the modern era from 1910 to the 1980s. It covers the Republic era (1910–1948), the People's Republic era (1949–1979) and the Globalization era (1980s to the present).

Note

1 The title of the National Games in Chinese is '中华人民共和国全国运动会'. It is generally known by a shortened form '全运会' in Chinese.

Acknowledgements

This research was supported by inspiring and insightful discussions with scholars and colleagues in both China and the United Kingdom. We would like to thank Professors Luo Shiming, Wang Yi, Tan Hua, Fan Wei, Mr. Michael Azariadis, and Professors Cao Shouhe, Xie Qionghuan, Xiong Xiaozheng, Ian Henry, Sun Qilin, Li Chongshen, Zheng Guohua, Wang Yan and Tan Tien-chin for their invaluable assistance to this research project. We are grateful for all of the people whom we interviewed, for sharing their experience, information and knowledge of the National Games, which helped us to understand the relationship between the National Games and nationalism in China. We wish to acknowledge the China Scholarship Council, University College Cork (UCC), the University of Western Australia (UWA), Anhui Normal University and Bangor University for their professional and financial support to this research. This work was supported by the Start-up Research Foundation for New Staff of Anhui Normal University (2017XJJ21).

Thanks also go to our fellow colleagues and PhD friends in China, Ireland, Australia and the UK. We wish you all well with your respective projects and careers. Last but not least, we appreciate the valuable support and encouragement from our family members. Without your unconditional love, we would never have come this far.

1 Modern Chinese nation, nationalism, national identity and sport

The evolution of the concept of a modern Chinese nation

Nation-building (or as it is sometimes called, state-building) is defined as a process of the construction of a national identity and a functioning state in which the citizens share the feeling of a commonality of interests, goals and preferences. The purpose of nation-building is to achieve the unification of the people within the state in order to remain politically stable and viable in the long run.[1] Questions of nation, nationalism or national identity are ubiquitous and pervasive in the modern world. The studies of nation, nationalism and national identity are multiple and varied across and within the academic world from different disciplines and perspectives.

Modern Chinese nation and Chinese nationalist consciousness was sparked by China's defeats in a series of wars against Western imperialists and Japan in the 19th century. The Chinese nation was a constructed notion that came about because 'the other' – the West – came into China, which pushed Chinese intellectuals to reconstruct 'the self' – the Chinese nation. According to Wang Zhongfu, the 'Chinese term for nation (民族) was introduced from Europe by Liang Qichao early in the 20th century. Since then, "nation" has been used widely in China'.[2] Chen Liankai describes how the notion of 'Chinese nation' was adopted from the writings of Meiji Japan and began to appear in Chinese revolutionary journals in 1895 in reference to the Han Chinese.[3] Zhang Taiyan was a Chinese writer who used the term 'Chinese people' for the first time in China and introduced the concept of 'Chinese people'. This marked the beginning of a modern concept of Chinese national identity.[4] However, in the early 20th century, 'Chinese nation' or 'Chinese people' was used as an ethnic term by Zhang Taiyan and other Chinese intellectuals to refer to Han Chinese, as Han people were ruled by the Manchu minority at the time.

After victory of the nationalist revolution in 1911 ended the Manchu rule, Chinese intellectuals and political leaders sought to build a unified nation-state that had equal status with other great powers in the world. The Chinese nation, as a political and cultural notion, was officially used by Sun Yat-sen in 1912 in Nanjing when he declared establishment of the Republic of China as a nation-state. In order to maintain most of the territory that was held under Manchu imperial rule, Sun Yat-sen and other nationalists in the Republic of China had to seek ways to live with and assimilate Manchu as well as other ethnic minorities into the Han-dominated modern nation-state.[5] For example, the notion of the Chinese nation officially included five identified ethnic groups: Han and other four major ethnic minorities – Manchu, Mongolian, Hui and Zang. It was called Wuzu Gonghe (五族共和, a republic of five ethnic groups). However, the Nationalist Party's policy of national assimilation failed to absorb all of the ethnic minorities within the territory of China into Han, the dominated Chinese nation.

Mao Zedong and the Chinese Communist Party (CCP) came to power in 1949 and proclaimed the founding of the People's Republic of China (PRC) in Beijing. The PRC officially describes itself as a 'unitary multinational state' under the slogan of 'the unity of nationalities'. The PRC claims that Chinese people are composed politically and culturally of 56 identified ethnic groups: Han majority and 55 other officially recognized ethnic minorities.[6] Although the other 55 ethnic minorities in China only make up a relatively small proportion of overall Chinese population, according to the national census, the Chinese government has established a series of policies to maintain equality and unity of ethnic groups and to ensure that Han and the other 55 minorities live in harmony.[7] For instance, the Chinese government allocates regional autonomy to ethnic minorities and respects and protects the languages, social customs and culture of ethnic minorities; the PRC has released a constitution and laws to protect the rights to economic and cultural development of all the ethnic minorities in China. These minorities enjoy preferential rights of exemption from population growth control of the 'One Child Policy', and ethnic minorities are represented in the National People's Congress as well as in governments at different levels. Thus, it can be seen that, after the fall of the Qing Dynasty in 1911, both the Nationalist Party and the CCP define the Chinese nation-state as a multiethnic political community and make an effort to construct the Chinese nation as a political and cultural community in order to maintain national unity.

Chinese nationalism and national identity

Chinese nationalism and national identity are also modern phenomenon, and the concept and origins of them are tangled with modern Chinese history of nation-building from the late Qing Dynasty at the beginning of the 20th century on. Joseph Levenson stated that culturalism permeated traditional Chinese thought and the ideology and identification of the mandarin were all forms of cultural consciousness.[8] Culturalism held China to be the only true civilization and embodied a universal value: people who accepted Chinese teachings and principles, including alien dynasties such as Mongo-Yuan and Manchu-Qing courts, could all be incorporated within its cultural bounds. China's defeat in the Opium War from 1840 to 1842 and subsequent humiliation at the hands of imperialist powers paved the way for disintegration of imperial China and led the Chinese elite to reject traditional culturalism and to borrow the Western concept of nationalism to defend China against foreign invasions in the late 19th century.[9] Thus, Chinese nationalism was born in the wreckage of culturalism and triggered by Western imperialists and imperial Japan's threat to China's territorial, cultural and even racial survival.

Nationalism was crucial to protecting and enhancing a strong sense of national identity and to maintaining national unity and nationhood, of national interests as well as territorial sovereignty during the process of nation-building. However, the content of nationalism was always changing in response to different situations in the political marketplace. Mario Ferrero declared that, 'the market for nationalism belongs in the same category as the market for social revolution or systemic change in general'.[10] The history of modern China was shaped by numerous national crises caused by both domestic turmoil and foreign aggression. Zhao Suisheng suggested that modern Chinese nationalism was shaped by national and social revolutions and its content was not eternal, yet 'situational' and 'in a state of flux, responding to the supply and demand conditions of a political market'.[11] In the realm of politics in modern Chinese history, Zhao classified Chinese nationalism into three categories: ethnic nationalism, liberal nationalism and state nationalism.[12] Zhao argues that:

> For ethnic nationalists, nationalism means building a single ethnic state. For liberal nationalists, it is a doctrine of social solidarity based on the symbols of nationhood, defined in terms of citizenship, political participation, and a common territory. For state nationalists, it is the desire to maintain the boundaries of the existing nation-state with its territory and population, to give the government the right to submit any objective to it, to reinforce its identity, and to justify the use of force to preserve its sovereignty against external as well as internal threats.[13]

In line with China's changing historical contexts, different political forces have turned to diversified types of nationalism as they connected with their own political values and interests. The chosen type of nationalism was imposed upon the rest of the population. For instance, ethnic nationalism was a mainstay of Chinese nationalism when the Han ethnic group led a state-seeking movement, or revolution, at the turn of 20th century, to oppose European imperialism as well as the minority Manchu rulers in the late Qing Dynasty. This was due both to defeat of China by the British imperialists in the Opium War and to the fact that the majority Han population struggled under the minority Manchu rulers. After the fall of the Qing Dynasty in 1911 and the founding of the Republic of China, the state elites soon encountered a contradiction between ethnic Han nationalism and the desire to keep all of the territories of the Qing Dynasty, including frontier areas where many ethnic minorities resided. To maintain a unitary multiethnic nation-state, Sun Yat-sen and other nationalist leaders in the Republic era rejected ethnic nationalism and constructed the Chinese nation-state as a multiethnic nation-state. This definition was accepted and developed in the PRC to maintain national unity among different ethnic groups within the Chinese territory.[14]

Liberal nationalism was introduced to China in the early 20th century. Liberal nationalists held a critical attitude towards authoritarian rule, so liberal nationalism sometimes offered up a challenge to the ruling party in both the nationalist and CCP regimes. A typical example was the Tiananmen Square Protests in 1989 in Beijing.[15] These liberal nationalists were liberals in the domestic arena and nationalists in the international arena, as they had a defensive attitude toward Western countries that imposed sanctions on China and, at the same time, they were critical of the CCP regime for violating their individual rights, which evolved into a challenge to the CCP's leadership. Thus, the Chinese government had to carefully suppress liberal nationalism in order to maintain its authority.

State nationalism, or state-led nationalism, was strongly advocated by incumbent political elites in both the regimes of the Nationalist Party and the CCP in China. State nationalism was similar to Jean-Dominique Lafay's notion of 'holistic view of nationalism', which regarded the state as

> a super-being, with its own aims and rights. This super-being is the sovereign judge of the national interest, and it has a natural right to promote this interest, whatever the consequence for the sovereignty and welfare of other nations or for the sovereignty and welfare of domestic individuals.[16]

Both the Nationalist Party and the CCP had the objective of building a centralized multiethnic nation-state in response to 'external threats to its sovereignty and internal challenges to its authority' to achieve national independence and state sovereignty as well as maintain the legitimacy of one-party rule.[17] However, the difference was, as Hunt stated, that the

Nationalist Party adopted a system-reforming approach in order to build a bourgeois state whereas the CCP adopted a system-transforming approach in order to build a worker's state.[18] Thus, the CCP developed a broader social base among the Chinese population and gained stronger nationalist credentials than did the Nationalist Party, which was eventually defeated by the CCP, who went on to establish the PRC in 1949.

Zhao Suisheng's definition of state nationalism, or state-led nationalism, was similar to today's Western's view of Chinese nationalism as 'party propaganda' that was politically constructed by the Nationalist Party or CCP.[19] Throughout the entire 20th century and the early years of the 21st century, all Chinese political leaders from Sun Yat-sen and Chiang Kai-shek, to Mao Zedong, Deng Xiaoping, Jiang Zemin, Hu Jingtao and Xi Jinping have shared a deep bitterness at China's humiliating losses of sovereignty to Western invasions in modern China. The propaganda of state-led nationalism in school history books and mass media has helped define the Chinese national identity over time. Even now, many educated Chinese people are still painfully aware of the unequal treaties signed with the Western powers or Japan, including the unequal treaties signed with the British at Nanjing in 1842 and with the Japanese at Shimonoseki in 1895. This state-led nationalism has been proved to be successful in encouraging Chinese people to work hard from generation to generation in order to blot out the past humiliation, to fight for China's rightful place in the world and to pursue the goal of national greatness (or the dream of a strong China) or peaceful rejuvenation.[20] This nationalism, however, has also produced 'xenophobia' towards foreigners in different historical contexts. When linked with China's international orientation, Zhao Suisheng has outlined three different nationalist perspectives: nativism, anti-traditionalism and pragmatism.[21]

According to Zhao's argument, nativists asserted that China's decline was primarily because of the foreign invasions, and China should eradicate foreign influences and return to Confucian traditions to revive its national strength.[22] For example, Mao Zedong's nativism is exemplified in his policy of Zili Gengsheng as well as militarization of the Chinese people in the first several decades of the PRC.[23] In contrast to nativism, anti-traditionalists called for a complete rejection of Chinese tradition since they considered China's tradition to be the source of its weakness and called for an unfettered adoption of certain Western models and culture, such as the imported socialist model in the early PRC and a hostile attitude towards all Chinese traditional culture during the Cultural Revolution from 1966 to 1976.[24] However, both nativist and anti-traditionalist nationalism lost ground due to their failure to revive China.[25]

Other than nativist and anti-traditionalist perspectives, pragmatic nationalism considered economic exploitation and cultural infiltration as the source of China's weakness and that the lack of modernization resulted in China's invasion by Western imperialism. Pragmatists in post-Mao China insisted on the adoption of whatever approach would achieve revitalization and economic modernization in China, and those who were pragmatic nationalists were more flexible in their tactics and subtle in their strategy.[26] This was well exemplified by Deng Xiaoping's saying, 'it does not matter if it is a black or white cat as long as it can catch rats'. Nevertheless, pragmatic nationalists were uncompromising with foreign demands involving China's vital interests and deeply committed to the preservation of national sovereignty, territorial integrity and attainment of national wealth and power. This was illustrated by the reversion of Hong Kong and Macao's sovereignty to China, China's Taiwan policy and China's claim to the Diaoyu Islands, as well as the South China Sea policy.

Moreover, the advocates of pragmatic nationalism acknowledged that nationalism was a double-edged sword.[27] The pragmatic state leaders in China consciously and continuously made efforts to cultivate this state-led pragmatic nationalism as a glue to unite the nation as well as to prevent the bottom-up nationalist sentiment of Chinese people from getting out of hand.[28] For example, in the 1990s, the Chinese government launched a nationwide Patriotic Education Campaign to promote pragmatic nationalism in the name of patriotism and to ensure loyalty in the population to the Chinese state and the CCP's leadership in China.[29] This state-led Patriotic Education Campaign officially defined 'the Chinese nation always as the total population of China, composed of 56 nationalities' and interpreted nationalism as 'love motherland or patriotism', which stressed that all Chinese people should love and support the PRC. This indicated the intention that promoting nationalism in the name of patriotism would avoid hurting the relationship between the Chinese government and ethnic minorities and could suppress ethnic nationalism in China in order to maintain the unity of a multiethnic Chinese nation-state.

Pragmatic nationalism was overshadowed by constant wars in the Republic of China era and also had an added overlay of Mao Zedong's Marxism-Leninism and self-reliance nativism in the early period of the PRC.[30] However, while nativism and anti-traditionalism continued to lurk in the background, pragmatic nationalism has been popular in China since the 1980s. It has become the dominant ideological instrument for political mobilization of the Chinese people and leadership. China has adopted a modernization strategy with the slogan 'building socialism with Chinese characteristics', which focused on marketing economic modernization. It has been stated that pragmatic nationalism is 'instrumental, state-led and reactive'.[31] The Chinese state-led pragmatic nationalism has been favoured since the 1980s by Chinese people of all walks of life, no matter how

uninterested they were in politics, because it has supported China's economic development and national unity in a relatively peaceful and stable
environment, both domestic and international.

Nationalism is crucial to the protection and enhancement of national
identity and national consciousness. China is a multiethnic nation-state
and it is important to have a strong sense of national identity to maintain
national unity and nationhood during the process of nation-building. The
Chinese government tries to build common cultural ties to construct an integrated Chinese national community. The common Chinese cultural symbols include the culture of the Han blended with culture from the other
55 minorities. The involvement of all cultural elements from ethnic groups
in China constructs and also enriches a common Chinese culture and shared
national identity. More importantly, this common culture is essential to the
building of a tightly unified and coherent national community. The symbols
and rituals include some traditional festivals, such as the Mid-autumn's Day
and the Spring Festival, and some ceremonies of mega-events, large-scale
expos and sports events at different levels.

Sport, nationalism and national identity

The inextricable relationship among nationalism, national identity and sport
has also attracted the interests of researchers since the 1980s, especially with
relation to mega-sports events, the Olympic Games, Asian Games, Commonwealth Games, Pan-Arab Games and Pan-American Games. Hobsbawm
identifies sport as a uniquely effective medium for inculcating nationalist
feelings and one of the most fertile sites for the construction, expression and
imagining of national identity; the imagined community of millions 'seems
more real as a team of eleven named people' with 'the unending succes-
sion of gladiatorial contests between persons and teams symbolizing state-
nations'.[32] It has been argued that sport can 'act in an important catalytic way
with respect to nationalism and national identity'.[33] Nationalism involves
promoting a country's culture and beliefs, establishing national identity and
demanding recognition and asserting dominance on an international level.[34]
National identity is regarded as one of the most marketable products in sport.
The involvement of government and politics is often motivated by a desire
for national prestige, and countries commonly attempt to assert dominance
through sport.[35]

Alan Bairner states that 'sport can be said to play a vital role in the construction and reproduction of the national identities involved'.[36] To explain
the relationship among sport, nationalism and national identity among
world nations in the new millennium, Bairner offers an analysis discussing
the relationship among sport, nationalism and national identities within the

context of globalization in the modern era in Europe and North America, Ireland, Scotland, Sweden, the United States and Canada. He proclaims that 'although the process known as globalization has clearly had an influence on them, the relationship between sport, national identity and nationalism remains as strong as ever'.[37] The persistence of nation-states under multiple formations of global culture has continued to involve the close intertwining of sport and nationalism.[38] Some observers insist that globalization is an ongoing process that has not yet awakened the relationship among sport, national identity and nationalism. Bairner provides some key insights into general links between sport and national identities and also offers the foundation upon which to construct the analyses of the relationship as it manifests itself in other nations.[39]

In the area of sport, national identity has been a major driving force in development in many countries, including the structure and funding of sport in the process of modern imperialist expansion, anti-imperialist resistance and contemporary nation-building projects. Namely, the ideology of nationalism, and in particular national identity, has made a vital contribution to the sports policies of many countries. Bairner focuses on two particular case studies (Ireland and Taiwan) to demonstrate the complex relationship among sport, nationalism and national identity in the post-colonial era in relation to sports development. For example, the Irish government put more emphasis (in terms of policy priority and funding) on developing the Gaelic Games and the Gaelic Athletic Association (GAA) in Ireland because the association played an important role in promoting Irish identity and resisting British colonialism.[40] The Taiwan case is much more complicated, but the development of baseball in Taiwan illustrates the influence of Japanese colonialism and American expansionism in Taiwan from 1895 to 1945. Thereafter, baseball was utilized by the ruling nationalist party from 1945 onward to enhance international visibility and construct a Chinese national identity so as to win the overseas Chinese people's support, consolidate its legitimacy, as well as Sinicize and enlist Taiwanese aboriginals.[41]

Houlihan analyzes the development of sport policy in Australia, Canada and the UK in the context of wider history and socio-politics for sport in general from the 1960s onwards. More specifically, he traces the development of elite sports policies and governance (national governing bodies of sport) in these three countries with the aim of achieving success at the Olympic Games and other international sports events. It is argued, for example, that the primary catalyst for Canada to put an increasing policy emphasis on elite sport was the urgent domestic concern with national identity. The Canadian government wanted to utilize international sports success as a symbol of Canadian national unity and to resist the growing influence of Quebec separatism on national politics.[42]

Moreover, building and strengthening national identity became a catalyst to trigger the refocusing on development of elite sport in many other countries in Asia, including China, South Korea, Singapore and Japan. For example, Japan's success in the 2004 Athens Olympic Games validated Japanese government's investment in its elite sports infrastructure and elite athletes. It also encouraged Japanese national elite sport policy actors to implement a number of initiatives to maintain its international sports success in recent years.[43] To promote progress of the island city-state, sport in Singapore has been utilized to foster social cohesion and national identity since its independence in 1965.[44] The Singapore government advocated a two-pronged approach to sport policy. On the one hand, it is centred on the well-being and collective benefits of exercise via mass sport participation; on the other hand, it is based on the ambition of having sports champions at international arenas. This was reemphasized by the former Prime Minister Goh Chok Tong when he said, 'the contribution of sports to nation-building and national pride is far-reaching. When Singapore athletes win medals at international sports competitions, they bring immense pride and joy to our people'.[45]

There are many arguments that strongly support Bairner's claim that 'nationalism flourish . . . national identities, at their best, make the world a more interesting and joyous place'.[46] Smith holds that within the sphere of nations and nationalism, politics and cultures have their own characteristics and their own patterns, which are totally different from those of economic systems. He also makes the point that nationalism in the contemporary world is significant to many people.[47] Anderson's idea of the 'imagined community' holds that the artificial characteristic of the nation relies to a large degree on myths, but as Bairner expresses 'it touches people's hearts and minds in ways that cosmopolitanism does not and may never be able to, regardless of the development of global economics, power structures, and cultural forms'.[48] In many cases, if a national state is facing a crisis, it will be threatened by alternative expressions of nationalism rather than by globalization. Smith suggested that 'national identity, as opposed to other kinds of collective identity, is pre-eminently functional for modernity, being suited to the needs of a wide variety of social groups and individuals in the modern epoch'.[49] Miller also asserts that national identity will retain its pervasive influence on people's behaviour.[50] While Anthony King concludes that both state and nation are undergoing a profound transformation, the state remains a critical political institution and the nation remains the primary social community.[51] Thus, it is obvious that the nation, nationalism and national identity coexist alongside globalization and are even strengthened by the process of globalization into the foreseeable future.

Furthermore, Michael Billig gives an insightful discussion on how nationalism is reinforced in people's everyday lives in *Banal Nationalism*.

Compared with Anderson's 'imagined communities', Billig uncovers how daily routines or imaginable subjects (including anthems, weather report maps, sports federations, the invention of traditions and cultures or many other mundane things) reinforced the public's concepts of national identity and nationalism. Namely, Billig states that 'the metonymic image of banal nationalism is not a flag which is being consciously waved with fervent passion; it is the flag hanging unnoticed on the public buildings'.[52] Sports events, sports arenas and the sports pages on newspapers well-illustrate that national identity is to be found in the embodied habits of social life in a familiar social environment.

The contribution of modern sport to nationalism and national identity has been widely studied since the 1980s, especially with regard to mega-sports events such as the Olympic Games, the FIFA World Cup, the Asian Games, the Commonwealth Games, and the Pan-Arabic Games.[53] The key question is why and how sport can arouse people from different social backgrounds to collaboratively support their nation's athletes and be integrated as one nation. One of the most important reasons is that sport involves interaction rituals that motivate the national sentiments of the nation.

Sport as a form of interaction ritual

Benedict Anderson has identified that interaction rituals are critical to the creation of imagined national communities. He points out that the printed mass media creates interaction rituals and is essential to the formation and transformation of the imagined community.[54] Individuals in the imagined community have no chance to meet all of the members, or even the majority of members, but the printed mass media, such as the newspaper, is a shared resource among a very wide social network. As such, it is employed across a nexus of interlocking interactions that unifies individuals within particular groups, and eventually a vast understanding is established across an entire nation and re-established constantly every day through massive trivial frequent interactions.[55] Thus, it is obvious that members of a nation can affirm their special relationships to one another by plenty of interaction rituals in their daily lives.

Many documents have explained why sport plays such an important role in promotion of nationalism or in the building of national identity. Research into and examinations of sport in multiracial states in European, American and Asian countries have clearly exemplified this relationship.[56] Anthony King claims that 'in England, football has become a shared public ritual which is central to popular imagination across the social hierarchy'.[57] James G. Kellas asserts that 'the most popular form of nationalist behaviour in many countries is in sport, where masses of people become highly emotional in support of their national team'.[58] Indeed, Grant Jarvie expresses that 'it is as if the imagined community or nation becomes more real on the terraces or the athletics tracks'.[59] Lincoln Allison argues that sport 'channels, releases, and even creates complex and powerful nationalist sentiments'.[60] Hargreaves also states that existing nation-states frequently use sport for a variety of purposes, including enhancing prestige, securing legitimacy, compensating for other aspects of life within their boundaries and pursuing international rivalries by peaceful means.[61] The interaction of sport and nationalism affects social, cultural and political domains, and the role of sport includes developing states, creating national identity and national rivalry; sport can 'reinforce patriotism, establish national consciousness, pride and unity and also be an instrument of national unity through the miscellaneous groups'.[62]

The means by which rituals are employed for political ends has been described and analyzed in great detail by David Kertzer.[63] Randall Collins has defined ritual as 'a mechanism of mutually focused emotion and attention producing a momentarily shared reality, which thereby generates solidarity and symbols of group membership'.[64] Collins also highlights the importance of interaction in generating emotion, a sense of belonging and identity, and he stressed the significance of emotion thus generated, particularly Durkheim's 'collective effervescence', in spurring groups of people to action.[65] Collins presents a detailed account of how rituals are constructed from a combination of ingredients, grow to differing levels of intensity and result in the outcomes of solidarity, symbolism and individual emotional energy. He puts forth a theory of how various interaction rituals generate myriad varieties of human social life. Collins gives four basic ingredients to define interaction rituals:

1　Two or more people are physically assembled in the same place, so that they affect each other by their bodily presence, whether it is in the foreground of their conscious attention or not.
2　There are boundaries to outsiders so that participants have a sense of who is taking part and who is excluded.
3　People focus their attention upon a common object or activity, and by communicating this focus to each other become mutually aware of each other's focus of attention.
4　They share a common mood or emotional experience.[66]

Where the ingredients combine and build up successfully, participants experience the four discernible outcomes as follows:

1　Group solidarity, a feeling of membership
2　Emotional energy in the individual: a feeling of confidence, elation, strength, enthusiasm and initiative in taking action

3   Symbols that represent the group: emblems or other representations (visual icons, words, gestures) that members feel are associated with themselves collectively; these are Durkheim's 'sacred objects'. Persons pumped up with feelings of group solidarity treat symbols with great respect and defend them against the disrespect of outsiders, and even more, of renegade insiders.
4   Feelings of morality: the sense of rightness in adhering to the group, respecting its symbols and defending both against transgressors. Along with this goes the sense of moral evil or impropriety in violating the group's solidarity and its symbolic representations.[67]

Competitive sport is considered by Collins to be a ritual 'contrived to produce situations of dramatic tension and victory', which generates emotional intensity among its spectators when the crowd collectively builds up a sense of anticipation and shared enthusiasm throughout the flow of events.[68] Sports competitions, as interaction rituals, are made use of by politics. Sports emblems and sports celebrities are sacred objects with the same function that Durkheim ascribes to a political leader who operates as an emblem for the crowd of which he or she is a centre of attention.[69] John Hargreaves holds that sports interaction ritual 'constitutes a powerful collective representation of the social and political order, focusing people's attention on the national symbols in a manner designed to invoke their loyalty'.[70] Collins points out that those sports events unconsciously and non-deliberately have all the natural elements for successful rituals. Sports events are 'normally scheduled, predictable, and contrived and they bring together a community that has no other coherence, and no other purpose, than the experience of the peaks of ritual emotion itself'.[71]

Thus, it can be seen that sport is sociologically important to nationalism because it constitutes a charged interaction ritual, not the only or the most important one, but perhaps the most striking ritual in the contemporary world.[72] These symbols and rituals in sports arenas help express and affirm a sense of nationalism and national identity for a national community. The mass media – print media, radio, television and Internet – broadcasts the sentiments in the sports arena to the whole of society, which enables more people to understand these symbols and rituals and to resonate with them. National symbols are mixed into the interaction rituals created by sport, which serves as a vehicle for promoting nationalism and the building of national identity in different imagined political communities. Among all the sports activities, the hosting of mega-sports events has a significant impact on the host nations or regions across a range of social, economic, political and cultural dimensions, particularly upon the project of political and cultural unity of an imagined community.

Chinese sport, nationalism and national identity

There is a growing body of literature on the relationships between Chinese sport and Chinese politics, or Chinese sport and Chinese nationalism, both in the West and in China. In the existing Chinese knowledge base, more studies have concentrated on the complex relationships between sport and politics from a macro historical perspective, especially with regard to how sport in China has played a significant role in the development of Chinese politics in modern and contemporary eras. Some also place particular focus on certain important landmark sports events. For example, a large number of journal articles and research projects have focused on the significance of China's involvement in international sports events, in particular the Olympic Games.[73]

In the existing Western knowledge base, more attention has been given to Chinese sport in the last few decades, in particular in the field of sport and Chinese political ideology or nationalism. For example, Jonathan Kolatch uncovers the subtle relationship between sport and political ideology in China and the important role of sport in the modernization of China.[74] Fan Hong points out that modern competitive sport was not a Chinese-born phenomenon, yet in China it has strong elements of nationalism and national identity. Sports events such as the Far East Championship Games (FECG, the forerunner of the Asian Games), the Games of the New Emerging Forces (GANEFO) and the Asian Games 'provided the Chinese sports community with the international perspective to form a conception of a sporting Chinese nation'.[75] Fan Hong and Xiong Xiaozheng examine how sport, as a political tool, has assisted with the implementation of political and diplomatic objectives in Communist China since 1949. Their analysis is undertaken from the perspective of some landmark sports events in China, such as the PRC's joining and breaking with the International Olympic Committee (IOC) in the 1950s, the PRC's involvement with the GANEFO in the 1960s, as well as the famous 'Ping-Pong Diplomacy' of the 1970s.[76]

Andrew D. Morris identifies the role of sports culture and ideology, Olympic-style competitions and the ball games as well as militarized forms of training, in the making of a modern nation-state in the Republican China.[77] Lu Zhouxiang and Fan Hong have explained why sport in China is so closely related to nationalism and patriotism and how sport is essential to the project of reviving the Chinese nation from both the macro and micro perspectives in the latest 150 years of Chinese history.[78] Xu Guoqi situates China's Olympic dream within the broader context of international relations and diplomacy from 1895 to 2008. His research helps us to understand China's 20th-century efforts to use sport to enhance its role and image in the international community and also in nation-building at home.[79] Many scholars other than Xu Guoqi also shed light on the influence of the 2008 Beijing Olympic Games on politics in China.[80] Susan Brownell articulates how sport occupies a critical place in body culture in China since sports events, such as the National Games, is an arena where the body as a cultural artifact is on display. She also uses a chapter to analyze the symbolism of the 1987 National Games in order to demonstrate the role of the National Games in the formation of a national consciousness and the consolidation of state power in the PRC.[81]

In addition to Susan Brownell's anthropological analysis of body culture in China through the lens of the 1987 National Games and her engagement with how changing types of public events reflect broader change in the symbolic construction of the Chinese state, several other researchers also give a brief account of the relationship between the National Games and Chinese politics. Fan Hong and Lu ZhouXiang introduce the 1959 National Games as one of the symbols of the Great Leap Forward of Sport in the PRC and highlight the 1965 National Games' contribution to Chinese politics and diplomacy. They also take the National Games to be an example of the role of sport in constructing the modern Chinese nation-state from 1912 to 1949. However, they do not provide further theoretical analysis as to how the National Games could construct a cohesive nationalist sentiment.[82]

Thus, from the previous research it has been determined that sport in China has a close relationship with politics and has been credited with helping modern and contemporary China to reconstruct Chinese people's confidence and to achieve a better internal and external image. Therefore, the demonstrated knowledge of nations and nationalism, sport and politics, sport and nationalism make a significant contribution to this research.

In this book, Zhao Suisheng's theories of Chinese nationalism are applied, in particular his notions of nativism, anti-traditionalism and pragmatic nationalism, to better understand evolution and development of Chinese top-down or state-led nationalism. Additionally, Randal Collins's interaction ritual theory, as well as Benedict Anderson's arguments on the interaction rituals created by the print media as the basis of imagined national communities, provide a theoretical underpinning to research that explores how the symbols and rituals of the National Games have contributed to and reinforced state-led Chinese nationalism and the making of the Chinese national identity from 1910 to 2009. Thus, a dynamic interrelationship is uncovered between the National Games and state-led nationalism as a political project in the process of nation-building in China.

In the light of socio-political context in China, the analysis of the National Games will be divided into three periods: the Republic period of China from 1910 to 1948, the early period of the PRC from 1959 to 1979 and the Reform and opening-up period from 1983 to 2009. In each period, the general information of the Games is given by presenting the themes, slogans, symbols, rituals and ceremonies of the Games, how the Games were managed and who was responsible for running them. The rituals of the National Games were witnessed by the competitors and spectators at the sports arenas and were also disseminated via mass media; interactions among the spectators (including the political leaders) and sports bodies created a strong emotional energy at the sports stadium. With the help of the mass media – print media, broadcast media, outdoor media, public speaking as well as the digital media of the Internet and mobile mass communication – these interactions between sports bodies and the audience in sports arenas formed charged interaction ritual chains with a strong emotional energy. These could easily be broadcast to different regions in China simultaneously and cost-effectively; hence, a high level of nationalist sentiment was created and shared among members of the Chinese nation as the games functioned as a metaphor of national desire, the nation-in-miniature, and projected an image par excellence of Chinese nationhood and national identity.

The National Games became integrated into part of the preparation for international competitions (in particular the Olympic Games), participation in which was seen to be characteristic of an independent nationhood and national identity. This objective was evident in the management of the Games in that most of the events were Olympic sports events, and the time and rules of the Games were in line with the Olympic Games. Despite that, the National Games in China displays strong elements of nationalism and national identity in its institutionalized rituals and ceremonies. The National Games drew the masses in and mobilized them in support of the cause of Chinese nation-building. Through the ideal platform of the National Games, the Chinese nation is represented and demonstrated. The flying of national flags, the wearing of national emblems and the playing of national anthems demonstrated the Chinese nation; national leaders and other politicians were part of the audience in the arenas, and the media featured athletes who were critical articulators of the construction and symbolic making of Chinese nationhood. This research into the reciprocal relationship between the National Games and nationalism and national identity from 1910 to 2009 is also a microcosm of the intertwined relationship between sport and politics at a broader level in modern and contemporary China.

Notes

1 Harris Mylonas, *The Politics of Nation-Building: Making Co-Nationals, Refugees, and Minorities* (Cambridge: Cambridge University Press, 2013).
2 Zhongfu Wang, 'Identification with History Versus Identification with Nation', *The Study of Chinese Culture* no. 25 (1999): 13.

3 Jinchun Han and Li Yifu, 'The Emergence of the Term "Minzu" in Chinese Language and Usage', *Nation Research* no. 2 (1984): 36–43.
4 Suisheng Zhao, *A Nation-State by Construction: Dynamics of Modern Chinese Nationalism* (Stanford: Stanford University Press, 2004), 46.
5 Ibid., 165–166.
6 Hongman Wang, *An Introduction to New China's Policy towards Minority Nationalities* (Beijing: Press of the Central University of Nationalities, 2000).
7 Dominant here refers to the population of Han nationality in China. The latest census in China was in 2010. The majority of China's population belongs to the Han Chinese (91.51%), whereas the 55 officially recognized minority nationalities account for about 8.49% of the total population. NBSC, China population census, 6th ed., 2011, www.stats.gov.cn/tjgb/rkpcgb/qgrkpcgb/t20110428_402722232.htm.
8 Joseph R. Levenson, *Confucian China and Its Modern Fate, Volume One: The Problem of Intellectual Continuity* (London: Routledge, 2013).
9 Mary C. Wright, ed., *China in Revolution: The First Phase, 1900–1913*, Volume. 237 (New Haven: Yale University Press, 1968), 3; Joseph B. R. Whitney, *China: Area, Administration and Nation-Building* (Chicago: University of Chicago, 1969), 26–29.
10 Mario Ferrero, 'The Economics of Socialist Nationalism: Evidence and Theory', in Albert Breton et al., eds., *Nationalism and Rationality* (Cambridge: Cambridge University Press, 1995): 208.
11 Zhao, *A Nation-State by Construction*, 20.
12 Ibid.
13 Ibid.
14 Ibid., 21–23.
15 It was a student-led popular demonstration in the form of anti-traditionalism and demanding democracy in Beijing in 1989.
16 Jean-Dominique Lafay, 'Conservative Nationalism and Democratic Institutions', in Albert Breton et al., eds., *Nationalism and Rationality* (Cambridge: Cambridge University Press, 1995): 163.
17 Zhao, *A Nation-State by Construction*, 26.
18 Michael H. Hunt, *The Genesis of Chinese Communist Foreign Policy* (New York: Columbia University Press, 1996), 55.
19 Peter Hays Gries, 'China and Chinese Nationalism', in Gerard Delanty and Krishan Kumar, eds., *The Sage Handbook of Nations and Nationalism* (London and Thousand Oaks: Sage, 2006): 488–499.
20 The rise of China is peaceful, as Yan Xuetong stated that, 'First, the Chinese regard their rise as regaining China's lost international status rather than as obtaining something new. . . . Second, Chinese consider the rise of China as a restoration of fairness rather than as gaining advantage over others'. Xuetong Yan, 'The Rise of China in Chinese Eyes', *Journal of Contemporary China* 10, no. 26 (2001): 34, 36.
21 Suisheng Zhao, 'Chinese Nationalism and Its International Orientations', *Political Science Quarterly* 115, no. 1 (2000): 1–33.
22 Zhao, *A Nation-State by Construction*, 251.
23 Zili Gengsheng, 自力更生, means Self-reliance, and it was Mao Zedong's policy of autarchy by isolating China completely from the rest of the world.
24 Although Mao Zedong acknowledged that some selected elements of Chinese traditional culture should be respected and used in a proper way, during the

Cultural Revolution, the Red Guards were directly against many prominent symbols of Chinese tradition in the name of destroying superstitions and feudal practices. Zhao, *A Nation-State by Construction*, 251.

25 Zhao, *A Nation-State by Construction*, 263.
26 Suisheng Zhao, 'China's Pragmatic Nationalism: Is It Manageable?', *The Washington Quarterly* 29, no. 1 (2005): 131–144.
27 Zhao, *A Nation-State by Construction*, 264.
28 Ibid., 265.
29 Suisheng Zhao, 'A State-Led Nationalism: The Patriotic Education Campaign in Post-Tiananmen China', *Communist and Post-Communist Studies* 31, no. 3 (1998): 287–302.
30 Zhao, *A Nation-State by Construction*, 209–211.
31 Zhao, 'Chinese Nationalism and Its International Orientations', 1–33.
32 Eric Hobsbawm, *Nations and Nationalism since 1780: Programme, Myth, Reality* (Cambridge: Cambridge University Press, 2012), 142–143.
33 Lincoln Allison, 'Sport and Nationalism', in Jay Coakley and Eric Dunning, eds., *Handbook of Sports Studies* (London and Thousand Oaks: Sage, 2000): 351.
34 Mike Cronin, *Sport and Nationalism in Ireland: Gaelic Games, Soccer and Irish Identity since 1884* (Dublin: Four Courts Press, 1999), 159.
35 Jay Coakley, *Sports in Society: Issues and Controversies* (New York: McGraw Hill, 2009).
36 Alan Bairner, *Sport, Nationalism, and Globalization: European and North American Perspective* (Albany: SUNY Press, 2001), 171.
37 Ibid., xi.
38 Lincoln Allison, ed., *The Global Politics of Sport: The Role of Global Institutions in Sport* (London: Psychology Press, 2005).
39 Bairner, *Sport, Nationalism, and Globalization*, xix.
40 Alan Bairner, 'Sports Development, Nations and Nationalism', in Barrie Houlihan and Mick Green, eds., *Routledge Handbook of Sports Development* (Oxon and New York: Routledge, 2011): 31–41.
41 Junwei Yu and Alan Bairner, 'Proud to be Chinese: Little League Baseball and National Identities in Taiwan during the 1970s', *Identities: Global Studies in Culture and Power* 15, no. 2: 216–239.
42 Mick Green and Barrie Houlihan, *Elite Sport Development: Policy Learning and Political Priorities* (London and New York: Routledge, 2005), 162.
43 Mayumi Ya-ya Yamamoto, 'Japan', in Barrie Houlihan and Mick Green, eds., *Comparative Elite Sport Development: Systems, Structures and Public Policy* (Oxford and Burlington, MA: Elsevier, 2008): 53–79.
44 Lion Teo, 'Singapore', in Barrie Houlihan and Mick Green, eds., *Comparative Elite Sport Development: Systems, Structures and Public Policy* (Oxford and Burlington, MA: Elsevier, 2008): 83–109.
45 SSC, *A Nation at Play: 25 Years of the Singapore Sports Council: Leading Sports into the 21st Century* (Singapore: SSC Publication, 1998), 74.
46 Bairner, *Sport, Nationalism, and Globalization*, 16.
47 Anthony D. Smith, *Nations and Nationalism in a Global Era* (Cambridge: Polity Press, 1995), 28.
48 Bairner, *Sport, Nationalism, and Globalization*, 16.
49 Smith, *Nations and Nationalism in a Global Era*, 155.
50 David Miller, *On Nationality* (Cambridge: Oxford University Press, 1995), 27.

51   Anthony King, 'Nationalism and Sport', in Gerard Delanty and Krishan Kumar, eds., *The Sage Handbook of Nations and Nationalism* (Thousand Oaks: Sage, 2006): 258.
52   Michael Billig, *Banal Nationalism* (London and Thousand Oaks: Sage, 2002), 119–122.
53   Bairner, *Sport, Nationalism, and Globalization*; Boria Majumdar and Hong Fan, eds., *Modern Sport: The Global Obsession: Politics, Religion, Class, Gender: Essays in Honour of JA Mangan* (London: Routledge, 2007); Mike Cronin and David Mayall, eds., *Sports Nationalisms: Identity, Ethnicity, Immigration and Assimilation* (London: Routledge, 2005); Ian P. Henry, Mahfoud Amara and Mansour Al-Tauqi, 'Sport, Arab Nationalism and the Pan-Arab Games', *International Review for the Sociology of Sport* 38, no. 3 (2003): 295–310.
54   Benedict Anderson, *Imagined Communities: Reflections on the Origin and Spread of Nationalism* (London: Verso Books, 2006).
55   King, 'Nationalism and Sport', 251.
56   Vic Duke and Liz Crolley, *Football, Nationality and the State* (Harlow: Longman, 1996); John Sugden and Alan Tomlinson, *Hosts and Champions: Soccer Cultures, National Identities and the USA World Cup* (Surrey: Ashgate, 1994).
57   King, 'Nationalism and Sport', 249.
58   James G. Kellas, *The Politics of Nationalism and Ethnicity* (London: Macmillan, 1998), 21.
59   Grant Jarvie, 'Sport, Nationalism and Cultural Identity', in Lincoln Allison, ed., *The Changing Politics of Sport* (Manchester: Manchester University Press, 1993): 75.
60   Allison, 'Sport and Nationalism', 354.
61   John Hargreaves, 'Olympism and Nationalism: Some Preliminary Consideration', *International Review for the Sociology of Sport* 27, no. 2 (1992): 119–135.
62   Mustafa Yaşar Şahin, Fatih Yenel and Tekin Çolakoğlu, 'Sport and Nationalism Interaction: Sports' Place and Importance Creating National Identity', *International Journal of Human Sciences* 7, no. 1 (2010): 1244–1263.
63   David I. Kertzer, *Ritual, Politics, and Power* (New Haven: Yale University Press, 1988).
64   Randall Collins, *Interaction Ritual Chains* (Princeton: Princeton University Press, 2004), 7.
65   Ibid.
66   Ibid., 48.
67   Ibid.
68   Ibid., 58.
69   Emile Durkheim, *The Elementary Forms of the Religious Life* (New York: Courier Dover Publications, 2012), 243–244.
70   John Hargreaves, *Sport, Power and Culture* (London: Routledge and Kegan Paul, 1986), 12.
71   Collins, *Interaction Ritual Chains*, 58–59.
72   Anthony King, *End of the Terraces: The Transformation of English Football* (London: Bloomsbury Publishing, 2002).
73   Zhi Chang and Yingjie Luo, 'Developing Perspective, Influencing Factors and Course of Sports Diplomacy of New China', *Sport Science* 24, no. 9 (2004): 12–15; Fenghua Yang and Kaizhen Wang, 'A Study of 2008 Olympic Games

on International Status and Reputation of Chinese Athletic Sports', *Journal of Beijing Sport University* 2, no. 5 (2008): 2–4; Hai Ren and Xianglin Luo, 'The Impacts of Beijing 2008 Olympic Games on China's Politics', *Journal of Sports and Science* 26, no. 2 (2005): 1–5; Li Zhu and Tang Pei, 'China's 60 Years of Sport Diplomacy: A Review and an Expectation', *Sports Culture Guide* no. 12 (2009): 140–145.
74 Jonathan Kolatch, *Sports, Politics, and Ideology in China* (New York: Jonathan David Publishers, 1972).
75 Hong Fan and James A. Mangan, eds., *Sport in Asian Society: Past and Present* (London: Routledge, 2005); Hong Fan, ed., *Sport, Nationalism and Orientalism: The Asian Games* (London: Routledge, 2013), xxi–xxiii.
76 Hong Fan and Xiaozheng Xiong, 'Communist China: Sport, Politics and Diplomacy', *The International Journal of the History of Sport* 19, nos. 2–3 (2002): 319–342.
77 The Olympic-style competitions that the Republican China had involved in included the International Olympic Games, the Far East Championship Games and the Chinese National Games. Andrew D. Morris, *Marrow of the Nation: A History of Sport and Physical Culture in Republican China* (Berkeley and Los Angeles: University of California Press, 2004).
78 Zhouxiang Lu and Hong Fan, *Sport and Nationalism in China* (London and New York: Routledge, 2013).
79 Guoqi Xu, *Olympic Dreams: China and Sports, 1895–2008* (Cambridge, MA: Harvard University Press, 2009).
80 Julia Lovell, 'Prologue: Beijing 2008 – The Mixed Messages of Contemporary Chinese Nationalism', *The International Journal of the History of Sport* 25, no. 7 (2008): 758–778; Xin Xu, 'Modernizing China in the Olympic Spotlight: China's National Identity and the 2008 Beijing Olympiad', *The Sociological Review* 54, no. 2 (2006): 90–107; Li Zhang and Simon Xiaobin Zhao, 'City Branding and the Olympic Effect: A Case Study of Beijing', *Cities* 26, no. 5 (2009): 245–254; Xuefei Ren, 'Architecture and Nation Building in the Age of Globalization: Construction of the National Stadium of Beijing for the 2008 Olympics', *Journal of Urban Affairs* 30, no. 2 (2008): 175–190; Fan Hong, Wu Ping and Xiong Huan, 'Beijing Ambitions: An Analysis of the Chinese Elite Sports System and Its Olympic Strategy for the 2008 Olympic Games', *The International Journal of the History of Sport* 22, no.4 (2005): 510–529; Susan Brownell, *Beijing's Games: What the Olympics Mean to China* (Washington, DC: Rowman & Littlefield, 2008); Monroe Price and Daniel Dayan, eds., *Owning the Olympics: Narratives of the New China* (Ann Arbor: University of Michigan Press, 2008); Ryan Ong, 'New Beijing, Great Olympics: Beijing and its Unfolding Olympic Legacy', *Stanford Journal of East Asian Affairs* 4, no. 2 (2004): 35–49.
81 Susan Brownell, *Training the Body for China: Sports in the Moral Order of the People's Republic* (Chicago: University of Chicago Press, 1995), 99–119.
82 Hong Fan and Zhouxiang Lu, 'Special Issue: Communists and Champions: The Politicization of Sport in Modern China', *International Journal of the History of Sport* 29, no. 1 (2012): 1–52; Zhouxiang Lu, 'Sport, Nationalism and the Building of the Modern Chinese Nation State (1912–49)', *The International Journal of the History of Sport* 28, no. 7 (2011): 1030–1054; Lu and Fan, *Sport and Nationalism in China*.

References

Allison, Lincoln, ed. *The Global Politics of Sport: The Role of Global Institutions in Sport*. London: Psychology Press, 2005.

Allison, Lincoln. 'Sport and Nationalism.' In *Handbook of Sports Studies*, edited by Jay Coakley and Eric Dunning, 344–355. London and Thousand Oaks: Sage, 2000.

Anderson, Benedict. *Imagined Communities: Reflections on the Origin and Spread of Nationalism*. London: Verso Books, 2006.

Bairner, Alan. 'Sports Development, Nations and Nationalism.' In *Routledge Handbook of Sports Development*, edited by Barrie Houlihan and Mick Green, 31–41. Oxon and New York: Routledge, 2011.

Bairner, Alan. *Sport, Nationalism, and Globalization: European and North American Perspective*. Albany: SUNY Press, 2001.

Billig, Michael. *Banal Nationalism*. London and Thousand Oaks: Sage, 2002.

Brownell, Susan. *Beijing's Games: What the Olympics Mean to China*. Washington, DC: Rowman & Littlefield, 2008.

Brownell, Susan. *Training the Body for China: Sports in the Moral Order of the People's Republic*. Chicago: University of Chicago Press, 1995.

Coakley, Jay. *Sports in Society: Issues and Controversies*. New York: McGraw Hill, 2009.

Collins, Randall. *Interaction Ritual Chains*. Princeton: Princeton University Press, 2004.

Cronin, Mike, and David Mayall, eds. *Sporting Nationalisms: Identity, Ethnicity, Immigration and Assimilation*. London: Routledge, 2005.

Cronin, Mike. *Sport and Nationalism in Ireland: Gaelic Games, Soccer and Irish Identity since 1884*. Dublin: Four Courts Press, 1999.

David, Miller. *On Nationality*. Cambridge: Oxford University Press, 1995.

Duke, Vic, and Liz Crolley. *Football, Nationality and the State*. Harlow: Longman, 1996.

Durkheim, Emile. *The Elementary Forms of the Religious Life*. New York: Courier Dover Publications, 2012.

Fan, Hong, ed. *Sport, Nationalism and Orientalism: The Asian Games*. London: Routledge, 2013.

Fan, Hong, and James A. Mangan, eds. *Sport in Asian Society: Past and Present*. London: Routledge, 2005.

Fan, Hong, and Xiaozheng Xiong. 'Communist China: Sport, Politics and Diplomacy.' *The International Journal of the History of Sport* 19, nos. 2–3 (2002): 319–342.

Green, Mick, and Barrie Houlihan. *Elite Sport Development: Policy Learning and Political Priorities*. London and New York: Routledge, 2005.

Gries, Peter Hays. 'China and Chinese Nationalism.' In *The Sage Handbook of Nations and Nationalism*, edited by Gerard Delanty and Krishan Kumar, 488–499. London and Thousand Oaks: Sage, 2006.

Han, Jinchun, and Li Yifu. 'The Emergence of the Term "Minzu" in Chinese Language and Usage.' *Nation Research* no. 2 (1984): 36–43.

Hargreaves, John. 'Olympism and Nationalism: Some Preliminary Consideration.' *International Review for the Sociology of Sport* 27, no. 2 (1992): 119–135.

Hargreaves, John. *Sport, Power and Culture*. London: Routledge and Kegan Paul, 1986.

Henry, Ian P., Mahfoud Amara, and Mansour Al-Tauqi. 'Sport, Arab Nationalism and the Pan – Arab Games.' *International Review for the Sociology of Sport* 38, no. 3 (2003): 295–310.

Hobsbawm, Eric. *Nations and Nationalism since 1780: Programme, Myth, Reality*. Cambridge: Cambridge University Press, 2012.

Hunt, Michael H. *The Genesis of Chinese Communist Foreign Policy*. New York: Columbia University Press, 1996.

Kellas, James G. *The Politics of Nationalism and Ethnicity*. New York: St. Martin's Press, 1998.

Kertzer, David I. *Ritual, Politics, and Power*. New Haven: Yale University Press, 1988.

King, Anthony. 'Nationalism and Sport.' In *The Sage Handbook of Nations and Nationalism*, edited by Gerard Delanty and Krishan Kumar, 249–259. Thousand Oaks: Sage, 2006.

King, Anthony. *End of the Terraces: The Transformation of English Football*. London: Bloomsbury Publishing, 2002.

Kolatch, Jonathan. *Sports, Politics, and Ideology in China*. New York: Jonathan David Publishers, 1972.

Lafay, Jean-Dominique. 'Conservative Nationalism and Democratic Institutions.' In *Nationalism and Rationality*, edited by Albert Breton et al., 160–172. Cambridge: Cambridge University Press, 1995.

Levenson, Joseph R. *Confucian China and Its Modern Fate: Volume One: The Problem of Intellectual Continuity*, Vol. 14. London: Routledge, 2013.

Lovell, Julia. 'Prologue: Beijing 2008 – The Mixed Messages of Contemporary Chinese Nationalism.' *The International Journal of the History of Sport* 25, no. 7 (2008): 758–778.

Lu, Zhouxiang, and Hong Fan. *Sport and Nationalism in China*. London and New York: Routledge, 2013.

Lu, Zhouxiang. 'Sport, Nationalism and the Building of the Modern Chinese Nation State (1912–49).' *The International Journal of the History of Sport* 28, no. 7 (2011): 1030–1054.

Majumdar, Boria, and Hong Fan, eds. *Modern Sport: The Global Obsession: Politics, Religion, Class, Gender: Essays in Honour of JA Mangan*. London: Routledge, 2007.

Morris, Andrew D. *Marrow of the Nation: A History of Sport and Physical Culture in Republican China*. Berkeley and Los Angeles: University of California Press, 2004.

Mylonas, Harris. *The Politics of Nation-building: Making Co-nationals, Refugees, and Minorities*. Cambridge: Cambridge University Press, 2013.

Şahin, Mustafa Yaşar, Fatih Yenel, and Tekin Çolakoğlu. 'Sport and Nationalism Interaction: Sports' Place and Importance Creating National Identity.' *International Journal of Human Sciences* 7, no. 1 (2010): 1244–1263.

Smith, Anthony D. *Nations and Nationalism in a Global Era*. Malden, MA: Polity Press, 2013.

SSC. *A Nation at Play: 25 Years of the Singapore Sports Council: Leading Sports into the 21st Century*. Singapore: SSC Publication, 1998.

Sugden, John, and Alan Tomlinson. *Hosts and Champions: Soccer Cultures, National Identities and the USA World Cup*. Surrey: Ashgate, 1994.

Teo, Lion. 'Singapore.' In *Comparative Elite Sport Development: Systems, Structures and Public Policy*, edited by Barrie Houlihan and Mick Green, 83–109. Oxford and Burlington, MA: Elsevier, 2008.

Wang, Hongman. *An Introduction to New China's Policy towards Minority Nationalities*. Beijing: Press of the Central University of Nationalities, 2000.

Wang, Zhongfu. 'Identification with History Versus Identification with Nation.' *The Study of Chinese Culture* no. 25 (1999): 13–15.

Whitney, Joseph B. R. *China: Area, Administration and Nation-Building*. Chicago: University of Chicago, 1969.

Wright, Mary C., ed. *China in Revolution: The First Phase, 1900–1913*, Vol. 237. New Haven: Yale University Press, 1968.

Xu, Guoqi. *Olympic Dreams: China and Sports, 1895–2008*. Cambridge, MA: Harvard University Press, 2009.

Xu, Xin. 'Modernizing China in the Olympic Spotlight: China's National Identity and the 2008 Beijing Olympiad.' *The Sociological Review* 54, no. 2 (2006): 90–107.

Yamamoto, Y. Mayumi. 'Japan.' In *Comparative Elite Sport Development: Systems, Structures and Public Policy*, edited by Barrie Houlihan and Mick Green, 53–79. Oxford and Burlington, MA: Elsevier, 2008.

Yan, Xuetong. 'The Rise of China in Chinese Eyes.' *Journal of Contemporary China* 10, no. 26 (2001): 33–39.

Yu, Junwei, and Alan Bairner. 'Proud to be Chinese: Little League Baseball and National Identities in Taiwan during the 1970s.' *Identities: Global Studies in Culture and Power* 15, no. 2 (2008): 216–239.

Zhao, Suisheng. 'China's Pragmatic Nationalism: Is It Manageable?' *The Washington Quarterly* 29, no. 1 (2005): 131–144.

Zhao, Suisheng. 'Chinese Nationalism and Its International Orientations.' *Political Science Quarterly* 115, no. 1 (2000): 1–33.

Zhao, Suisheng. *A Nation-State by Construction: Dynamics of Modern Chinese Nationalism*. Stanford: Stanford University Press, 2004.

Zhao, Suisheng. 'A State-Led Nationalism: The Patriotic Education Campaign in Post-Tiananmen China.' *Communist and Post-Communist Studies* 31, no. 3 (1998): 287–302.

2 The origin and development of the National Games in the late Qing Dynasty and the Republic of China, 1910–1948

Introduction

Sport has been widely acknowledged as having made a significant contribution to the development of nationalism and national identity in China. This is especially true of mega-sports events.[1] The National Games were held in modern China seven times from 1910 to 1948 (see **Appendix 1**). The First National Games in Nanjing was initiated by the Shanghai Young Men's Christian Association (YMCA) in 1910 on the eve of the birth of the Republic of China (in 1912). After the founding of the Republic of China, another six National Games were held at irregular intervals in Beijing in 1914, Wuchang in 1924, Hangzhou in 1930, Nanjing in 1933, and Shanghai in 1935 and 1948. The objective of this chapter is to examine the social context, motivation and purpose of the National Games in the Republic of China and to explore the complex relationship between the National Games and nationalism, and the creation of a national consciousness and national identity. This will be explored through the analysis of the origin and development of the National Games from 1910 to 1948.

This chapter begins with a discussion of how Western sport was introduced to China in the modern era and how China gradually accepted Western sports ideology, which was different from China's inherent physical culture. The second section examines the birth of the National Games in China and highlights how this event was established by the Western missionary institution, the YMCA. It also explores how China regained the sovereignty of sport from the hands of Westerners by hosting the Third National Games in 1924. It shows that although the origin of the National Games had nothing to do with Chinese nationalism or national identity, and, to some degree, sport was regarded as cultural imperialism of the West in China, the Games taught the Chinese nationalists the value of sport in national salvation and nationhood. The third section explores the development of the National Games in the 1930s and 1940s and discusses the interplay of the rituals and symbols of the National Games and Chinese nationalism in the context of political and economic perspectives under the nationalist government in the Republic era. It concludes that the promotion of the National Games met the demands of China's national salvation and the principles of Chinese nationalism, such as sovereignty, territorial integrity and patriotic sentiment, in the decades of wars and political unrest. It argues that the National Games in the Republican China era played a role that was more significant than that of a sports event: it had a major influence in shaping Chinese independent nationhood and national identity.

The diffusion of modern Western sport to China

In the middle of the 18th century, China was doubtless one of the most advanced countries on earth with its secular political and social circumstance.[2] However, the Manchu power had already passed its apogee by the end of the 18th century. The country was 'externally strong but internally shriveled (外强中干)' and could not escape from the falling dynastic fortune with its serious administrative, military and moral problems.[3] However, the Chinese elite showed less interest in international affairs and were self-satisfied with the great power of their emperor, whose legitimacy or mandate to rule the vast Chinese empire derived from the belief that he was the 'Son of Heaven (天子)' on Earth and, as such, he owned the 'Tianxia (天下)', a territory ruled by the emperor. The term 'Tianxia' was a concept bigger than 'country'.[4] This is why China was called the Celestial Empire and why the emperor thought China was the only true civilization in the world whose cultural superiority remained unchallenged.[5] The insularity of China's Qing Dynasty rulers eventually witnessed how China's door was forced to open to Western countries by cannons and guns. China's defeat in the two Opium Wars (1840–1842, 1856–1860) forced the Celestial Empire to realize that China was no longer a dominant power in the world.[6] The Westerners landed in China and brought their own cultures and tastes, part of which included sport, to Chinese society.

Western sports, such as horse racing, cricket, soccer, rowing, hunting, track and field, were cumulatively popular after an increasing number of businessmen, soldiers, missionaries, administrators and diplomats chose to reside in different leased territories in cities of China, for instance in Shanghai, Ningbo, Fuzhou, Xiamen, Guangdong, Tianjin and Hankou. In these concessions, the Westerners were self-governed rather than being administered by the Chinese government. Their leisure pursuits included various sports activities. Some sports, such as cross-country running and long-distance speed-walking, required a lot of space, but some of the established sports stadiums, for instance in the Shanghai leased territories, could not meet their needs. Some sports were taken out of the leased territories and, for the first time, the Chinese people got the opportunity to personally witness the excitement of Western sport.[7] These sports activities were fresh and attractive to ordinary Chinese people and gave them the opportunity to see and learn how to take part in these activities.

Sports activities in missionary schools were another significant influence in assisting the introduction of Western sport to Chinese society. After 1850, a large number of missionaries came to China to proselytize. They built missionary schools to reinforce the power of the Church in order to promote Christianity in China. Some missionaries, however, had had a positive influence on, and made valuable contributions to, the import of Western culture, education and especially sport.[8] At the end of the 19th century, there were already approximately 2,000 missionary schools in China – including primary schools, secondary schools and colleges – with more than 40,000 Chinese students graduating from these schools. In the late 19th century, these missionary schools organized sports events, mainly on track and field. For instance, St John's University (formerly St John's College)[9] was a missionary school in Shanghai that held the first track and field competition in China. Between 1904 and 1908, the Chinese University Sports Federation, organized by St John's University, Suzhou Soochow University, Nan Yang Public School (founded in 1896 and the predecessor of Shanghai Jiao Tong University) and the Anglo-Chinese College, held track and field competitions five times. Later, the students in missionary schools were the main participants in the First, Second and Third National Games.[10]

The Young Men's Christian Association (YMCA) played a prominent role in organizing Western physical education and sports events in the Republican era.[11] In 1876, the first YMCA in mainland China was founded in Shanghai. In the early period of the 20th century, the number of YMCAs grew rapidly. In 1922, 17 provinces had YMCAs. This included 30 YMCAs in cities and 170 YMCAs within schools. Sports activities and events were effective ways for the YMCA to reach out to the young Chinese. From 1908 the North American YMCAs dispatched their sports directors to cities such as Beijing, Shanghai and Tianjin to provide physical education courses and training for physical education teachers who were to work in Chinese schools and local communities.[12] Moreover, the YMCA introduced the concept of modern Western sport and organized sports competitions. At the same time, the YMCA built gymnasia and nurtured young Chinese athletes. For instance, basketball, baseball, softball, tennis and table tennis were all popularized in China by the YMCA. Modern sports events provided the Chinese, especially young people, with the experience of participating in and organizing mega-sports events.

The YMCA also selected promising Chinese students to study at Spring-field College, Massachusetts, which was regarded as the headquarters of the training of YMCA physical education instructors in North America. At the same time, the Chinese government also sent students abroad to gain formal training in physical education. Between the end of the 19th century and early 20th century, the Qing government sent a large number of students to study overseas in Europe, America or Japan, and some overseas students specialized in physical education.[13] When they returned to China, they worked as educators and physical educators in universities. Most of them passionately promoted modern Western sport in Chinese society.

In summary, modern Western sport came to China through the channels of the missionary schools, the YMCA, Western agents such as missionaries, traders, soldiers, administrators and diplomats, as well as through Chinese overseas students. The question is why China was receptive to Western sport, a representation of Western ideology, which differed greatly from traditional Chinese physical culture.

Since the mid-19th century, China had been weakened not only by natural disasters, domestic unrest, and widespread opium addiction but also by successive invasions by Western powers such as the United Kingdom, Germany, France, and invasions from Russia and Japan. China had, at one point, been referred to as 'the sick man of Asia', both politically and physically.[14] This situation worried many Chinese intellectuals. They realized that the weaknesses of the Chinese nation were more than economic or military; in fact, they were inherent in the poor physical condition of its populace. Many Chinese intellectuals emphasized the importance of improving people's physiques. Liang Qichao, one of the most influential patriots and reformists, stated in *Qingyi Bao*[15] in 1899:

> the foreign education system includes Physical Education and that is the main reason that the Westerners are stronger in physique and mind. They are not threatened by enemies or defeated by other nations easily. They are brave enough to face the bloody massacre . . . so physical education is important both in strengthening body and mind. . . . Chinese people should support more young men to participate in military sport in China.[16]

The Chinese revolutionary and the foremost pioneer of the Republic of China, Sun Yat-sen professed that a powerful nation played a key role in establishing a strong country. Western-trained Sun Yat-sen and his Tong-menghui Chinese Revolutionary Alliance spearheaded the 1911 Revolution that overthrew the Qing Dynasty and proclaimed China to be a Republic in 1912.[17] Sun's nationalistic and democratic revolution was based on his famous revolutionary philosophy, Three People's Principles : (1) People's National Consciousness, or Nationalism; (2) People's Rights, or Democracy; and (3) People's Livelihood, or Socialism.[18] Sun's first principle, nationalism, not only called for 'the overthrow of the alien Manchu rule, but also the removal of the foreign imperialistic yoke'.[19] He also recommended that Chinese people should exercise more to develop a strong body to defend themselves and their nation. He realized that sport had a role to play in the health of the nation-state. Sun Yat-sen valued sport and saw its potential to strengthen Chinese soldiers' bodies so they could better serve the nationalist revolution.[20]

The 1919 May Fourth Movement[21] sparked national protests and marked the upsurge of modern Chinese nationalism. This was also partly considered to be a cultural revolution as well as a social movement.[22] A number of intellectuals had discussed the importance of sport and also promoted military training and physical education in schools, not only Chinese indigenous sport, but also Western sport. Cai Yuanpei, president of Peking University, advocated that sport would not only cultivate the mind but also prepare Chinese people for military service.[23] Tao Xingzhi,[24] a renowned Chinese educator in the 20th century, gave sport the pre-eminent position in the promotion of fitness. He stated that

> health is particularly important in the critical moment of a nation . . . and now is the important moment for China and if our nation wants to survive, we should militarize our nation as soon as possible. . . . Through sport, everyone can get a strong body and when the enemies come, we can defend our motherland.[25]

Since the 1920s, traditionalists in the Republic of China linked Chinese martial arts to the national revival. They renamed martial arts 'national arts (国术)' and attempted to reshape it to fit in with Western sport. Men's martial arts were included in all of the National Games since the Third Games in 1924, and women's martial arts were also demonstrated since the Fifth and subsequent Games. The martial arts were scheduled into mass displays and 'stamped with an official ideology that explicitly linked them with republican nationalism'.[26] Due to inadequate rules and safety measures, there were many serious injuries during the real competition, and it proved difficult to 'sportize' the martial arts. Later, in the 1930s, there was an important debate among Sinic nationalists, which was called Tuyangzhizheng (土洋之争) in China. This debate focused on whether China should accept Western sport or insist on Sinic indigenous sport as a symbol of modernization of physical culture. Many politicians, educators and sports experts were involved in the debate. Finally, the Chinese pragmatic nationalists won the debate.

The involvement in Western sport in many respects was regarded as a quasi-revolutionary action because modern Western sport was considered as an arena and a symbol of the breaking relationships with the traditional outdated society and the embracing of the egalitarian norms of modern society. The use of foreign methods to defeat foreign barbarians was needled into Chinese anti-imperialist nationalism, and this idea was favoured by Chinese nationalists. Modern Western sport was incorporated into the Chinese sports system as a symbol of Chinese modern culture.[27] From then on, China has been on its way to pursuing a Westernized idea of physical modernity, which emphasized the ideas of physicality, muscularity as well as active participation into sport. The mainstream of Chinese sport was not only the indigenous martial arts or traditional Chinese sports, but also Western athletics and ball games. The following sections discuss how the National Games came into being in the Late Qing period and how they were developed in the Republic of China from 1910 to 1948.

The YMCA and the birth of the National Games in 1910

In 1910, during the late Qing Dynasty, Max Joseph Exner,[28] a physical educator director of the Shanghai YMCA, together with the Shanghai YMCA, decided to organize a sports meet in the name of 'the First China National Athletic Meet' among schools in China. In the announcement, the YMCA emphasized that the sports meet was to copy the modern Olympic Games and to promote the Olympic movement in China.[29] To give supervision for the Games, Exner and the Shanghai YMCA established a temporary national sports committee called the First National Athletic Alliance of Regional Student Teams. Members of this sports committee were all from YMCAs in China, including eight Chinese and eight Westerners.[30]

This sport meet was held on the grounds of the Nanyang Industrial Exposition in Nanjing from 18–22 October 1910. It was one of the programmes for the Exposition to increase its influence.[31] It was China's first modern sports event at a national level, with 140 male athletes participating. Athletes came from five regions of China: three metropolitan regions (Shanghai, Nanjing and Suzhou, Wuhan), South China and North China. It included four of the recently introduced Western sports: athletics, tennis, football and basketball, and participants were divided into three different groups, including the senior group which was open to all, one group of college students, and a group of students from middle school.[32] Most of the participants were students from missionary schools or YMCA schools, such as Shanghai St John's University, Shanghai Nanyang Public School, Tianjin YMCA Board School, Tianjin Industry College, Wuchang Bowen College, Beijing Xiehe Academy and other middle schools sponsored by missionaries and YMCAs in China.[33]

It was reported that this sports meet attracted nearly 40,000 spectators each day.[34] After four days of competition, Shanghai was the champion of the senior group, and North China was the winner of the group of students from middle schools. For the group of college students, St John's University won first place, Nanyang Public School got second, and Tianjin YMCA Board School took third place.[35] De Wachter stated that 'modern sport is a mirror of modernity'.[36] The organization of this competitive sport not only represented Western cultural imperialism, but it was also symbolic of the modernity in Chinese society. However, this sports event technically could not be considered a nationwide event because the athletes were all male, the official language of the Games was English and the rules were conducted in English.[37] Yet it showed that sport in China had made a transition from traditional to modern Western sport. This sports meet was subsequently regarded as the First National Games by the nationalist government in the Republican era.

The YMCA and the second National Games in 1914

Four years later, on 21 and 22 May 1914, the Beijing YMCA utilized a public area near the Temple of Heaven as a sports arena to stage another sports event. This was called the First National United Athletic Meet (it was conventionally regarded as the Second National Games in the Republican era). The event was nominally hosted by the new sports organization, the Beijing Athletic Association, which had a close relationship with the Beijing YMCA. The person in charge of the Second National Games was Amos N. Hougland, a physical educator director of the Beijing YMCA.[38] Most of the referees of the games were Westerners from YMCAs in China, and only the chief and the honorary chief referees were Chinese; however, it was the beginning of the indigenization of Western sport in China.

Through preliminary meets, approximately 96 athletes were selected in each section to represent four regions: the East, the West, the South and the North of China. These sections were divided into different colours to represent these four regions: yellow, red, green and white.[39] There were six competitive sports: track and field, football, baseball, volleyball, basketball and tennis. Baseball and volleyball were projected as competition programme, to show a forging sense of the team spirit. Unlike the First National Games, this sports event did not divide athletes into different categories: it was open to all schools in China rather than confined to the missionary schools or the YMCAs in China. However, most schools in China were unfamiliar with Western sport, let alone the notion of a sports meet. This meant that most of the 96 male athletes came from missionary schools and the YMCAs in China.

Compared to the First National Games, this two-day competition was spectacular. It attracted about 15,000 spectators on the first day, but there was a sharp reduction in crowd numbers on the second day, as most of the audience was made up of privileged college students. The Beijing YMCA invited an American sports team to give a volleyball performance to show the Chinese audience the importance of teamwork and sportsmanship in sports events. Yuan Shikai, the first president of the Republic of China in Beijing, sent a government official to address the crowd, and the Presidential Palace Marching Band gave a performance at the closing ceremony.[40] Finally, the athletes from North China finished in first place.

Most Chinese people had never heard or seen these two games before, never mind be involved in them. It can therefore be interpreted that the birth of the National Games in China had nothing to do with Chinese nationalism or Chinese national identity; rather, it was a presentation of Western imperialism in China, albeit from the hand of Western missionaries. Yet the crowning achievements of the YMCA in China were to plant the seed of China's interest in modern Western sport, to introduce an understanding of sportsmanship and to emphasize the importance of physical and mental strength. The YMCA also initiated the earliest sports administrative organizations in China.[41] For example, in light of the inaugural of the first Chinese national sports event, the First National Athletic Alliance of Regional Student Teams was established in 1910. China's first nationwide sports organization – the China National Amateur Athletic Union – was established by the YMCA in 1922, which laid the foundation for the later establishment of the national sports organization by the Chinese themselves. Therefore, it can be interpreted that these two sports events were the achievement of the YMCA and the representation of Western imperialism in China. However, the Chinese nationalists and sports leaders became increasingly aware of this situation and of the lack of sports sovereignty in China.

Sports sovereignty and the Third National Games in 1924

Benedict Anderson termed a nation as 'an imagined political community', which pointed to the process of a nation or any social group coming into being.[42] The existence of a nation relied on its members' recognition of their common bond and their understanding of shared interests and duties.[43] Anderson also identified 'a daily ritual as an exclusive period of interaction which has been critical to the creation of imagined communities'.[44] Sport was important to nations and nationalism because it 'constitutes a charged interactive ritual out of which imagined national communities arise'.[45] Sport has proven to be one of the most important rituals that can affirm the networks that constitute a nation,[46] and sport 'channels, releases, and even creates complex and powerful nationalist sentiment'.[47] In addition, Maurice Roche argued that sports events often have significant long-term pre-event and post-event impacts on the host nation across the cultural, political and economic dimensions of national society.[48]

The First and Second National Games in 1910 and 1914 in China were organized by the YMCAs in China. The official language of the Games was English, and the rules were conducted in English. Even China's six involvements in the Far Eastern Championship Games (FECG) from 1913 to 1923 were led by Westerners in China. This was considered a national embarrassment, or even a national humiliation, by Chinese nationalists and politicians alike.[49] The failure of the Chinese sports delegation at the Sixth FECG triggered Chinese nationalists and sports experts to eagerly seek out solutions to take back sports sovereignty from the control of Westerners. They valued the sports event and saw its potential to display the 'Chinese people's body' in order to get rid of the humiliating title, 'the Sick man of East Asia'. Through the rituals of sport, the Chinese people could be mobilized and consolidated into a collective sense of belonging to the nation.[50] Furthermore, the nationalists professed that a national sports event offered a vision of symbolic, participatory and celebratory national community.[51]

Therefore, Chinese nationalists seized the opportunity to host the Third National Games in 1924 whilst efforts were being made by local sports organizations in the provinces to establish a national sports organization. Eventually, the China National Amateur Athletic Federation (CNAAF) was founded on 3 April 1924. This was China's first national sports organization initiated by Chinese, and all members in the CNAAF were Chinese.[52] Later, with the support of the local government, the Third National Games, the first Chinese-run National Games, was held from 22 to 24 May 1924 in Wuchang, Hubei province and staged at the Hubei Public Grounds in Wuchang city. It marked the beginning of China's self-governance of its own sports mega-event.[53] To some extent, the Third Games turned out to be a turning point in the process of indigenizing Western sport, in particular Western competitive sport in China.

Xiong Xiling (熊希龄)[54] was honoured as the president of the Third National Games in 1924 and Zhang Boling[55] was the chief referee. Most of the referees in this competition were Chinese except for three foreign referees in swimming and baseball. The unit of measurement for the track and field events changed from yards to metres, which is still used in sport in China. The official language of the Games was Chinese and the rules were translated into Chinese.[56] There were about 340 athletes from five regions of China, including East China (Jiangsu and Zhejiang), West China (Gansu, Shaanxi, Sichuan, Yunnan and Guizhou), South China (Canton, Fujian and Guangxi), North China (Zhili, Henan, Shandong, Shanxi and other north-eastern provinces) and Central China (Hubei, Hunan, Anhui and Jiangxi).[57] Athletes from different regions in China were selected through many preliminaries organized by the preparation committee so that the number of athletes was much greater than in the previous two games.[58] They participated in seven competitive sports: athletics, swimming, football, basketball, volleyball, baseball and tennis. It was the first National Games to have women's events, but only for exhibition purposes. Women's sports teams from Hubei, Hunan, Jiangxi and Jiangsu provinces demonstrated their skills in basketball, volleyball and softball. It also clearly illustrated the new face of modern Chinese women, who had strong bodies and strong minds. Chinese martial arts appeared for the first time as part of the demonstration programme to exhibit the indigenous national physical culture. In addition, modern technology was used for the first time at this sports event; for example, a field telephone system was installed to deliver messages throughout the grounds.[59]

Although China was locked in the Warlord Era (1916–1928), the nationalist government in Beijing still sent governmental officials to deliver congratulatory speeches at the opening ceremonies of the Third Games in 1924, which showed the government's support and highlighted the significant role of sport in strengthening the bonds of Chinese nationhood. Their speeches were printed and passed out to the audiences. The major theme of their speeches expressed the revitalization of national power through sport. Zhang Ziqi (张子奇), a member of the Bureau of Investigation and Statistics in the Republic of China, commented that:

> the Third National Games finally got rid of control of the Western missionaries; this sports event was arranged by the Chinese and the results of this games were spectacular. . . . It was well equipped and highly supported by Chinese people; so strictly speaking, it was wonderful that the Third National Games was a great success because this was the first time for our nation to organize nationwide sports event by our own Chinese people.[60]

This three-day competition was a success, despite happening during such a turbulent time. Athletes from North China won first place, followed by East China and Central China. Compared to the first two Games, the spectators of the Third Games included people from all walks of life. These games also reflected Chinese people's changing view towards modern Western sport, from little knowledge of it to its gradual acceptance and practice. The Third National Games in 1924 assisted and witnessed the indigenized process of modern Western sport in Chinese society. Moreover, with the help of publicity from politicians, scholars and the newspaper media, the

Third National Games bound people to protect Chinese sovereignty, which resulted in the promotion of national confidence, national consciousness and patriotic nationalism.

The National Games under the Nanjing nationalist government

In March 1927, the nationalist government shifted its political centre from Beijing to Nanjing. The support of a sports event in nation-building and maintaining nationhood had resonance among the nationalists in China, and the involvement of the Nanjing nationalist government was conducive to the growth of modern sport in China. From 1928 to 1935, the Fourth, Fifth and Sixth National Games were organized by the CNAAF and supported by the nationalist government (see Table 2.1).[61] This facilitated the quick development of the National Games in the Republican era in a relatively stable national environment. For instance, the nationalist government funded the construction of the sports stadium and other infrastructures for the Games: the Zhejiang Sports Stadium in Hangzhou for the Fourth National Games in 1930, the Nanjing Central Stadium for the Fifth National Games in 1933 and the Shanghai Jiangwan Sports Stadium for the Sixth National Games in 1935. The increased number of athletes and delegations demonstrated the progress of the National Games, and these delegations reflected the administration divisions, cities and provinces throughout China. The number of delegations increased from 22 at the Fourth National Games to 38 at the Seventh National Games, and the number of athletes grew rapidly, from 1,627 at the Fourth National Games in 1930 to 2,286 at the Sixth National Games in 1935. Female athletes had been attending formal competitive events since the Fourth National Games in 1930, and Chinese martial arts had officially become part of the competitive programme since the Fifth National Games in

Table 2.1 The National Games between 1910 and 1948 in Republican China[62]

National Games	Date	Host city	Sports	Delegations	No. of Athletes
1	18–22 October 1910	Nanjing	4	5	140
2	21–22 May 1914	Beijing	6	4	96
3	22–24 May 1924	Wuchang	7	4	340
4	1–10 April 1930	Hangzhou	12	22	1,627
5	10–22 October 1933	Nanjing	17	30	2,248
6	10–22 October 1935	Shanghai	17	38	2,286
7	5–16 May 1948	Shanghai	18	58	2,677

Source: Compiled by the authors.

1933. The performance of the athletes showed the progress of modern sport in China. For example, at the Fifth National Games in 1933, the sprinter Liu Changchun created a new national record of the 100 metres in a time of 10.7 seconds, which was close to the elite level in the world at the time. At the Sixth National Games in 1935, eleven national records in track and field athletics and eight national records in swimming were broken. During this time, these National Games were known by many Chinese people, and many school students in local China attended the preliminaries of the Games. For example, more than 10,000 spectators watched 3,000 primary school students perform t'ai chi at the opening ceremony of the Sixth National Games.[63] In addition, in line with the nationalist government's requirement, some newspapers and illustrated magazines published special issues during the Games, including *Shen Bao, Liangyou Huabao, Beiyang Huabao* and *Meishu Shenghuo*.[64]

After the Sixth National Games in 1935, the Ministry of Education issued seven regulations on the National Games:

> In order to promote sport, the National Games will be held every two years in capital city Nanjing or other cities in different provinces in turns (for example, the fifth National Games was held in the capital city Nanjing and the sixth in Shanghai; the Seventh National Games will be held in Nanjing and the eighth will be held in another city).[65]

According to this announcement, the Seventh National Games should have been held in Nanjing in 1937, yet due to the Second Sino-Japanese War (1937–1945), the National Games had to be suspended for 13 years. To host another national sports event in 1948 was regarded as an opportunity for the nationalist government to inspire Chinese national spirit after the anti-Japanese war.[66] The nationalist government organized the Seventh (the last) National Games in Republican China from 5–16 May 1948 at Shanghai Jiangwan Sports Stadium. There were 2,677 athletes from 55 delegations, including Taiwan, the Northeast of China, which was captured by Japan for 14 years, and the delegations of overseas Chinese. Taiwan, for the first time in history, attended this meeting because it had been occupied by Japan after the first Sino-Japanese War in 1895 and was returned to China after the Second Sino-Japanese War in 1945.[67]

Compared to the Fifth and Sixth Games, the performance of athletes of the Seventh Games was declined. This can be explained as, during this period, China and the Chinese people had suffered from wars and economic distress. However, with the support of the nationalist government, the National Games from 1930 to 1948 made its development and witnessed the changing attitude of the modern Western sport in China. Although China faced its difficult time of anti-Japanese war, these National Games under the nationalist government in Nanjing served as a way of uniting the entire nation to express and affirm nationhood in the Republican Era.

Rites and symbols of the National Games

Symbolic rituals are designed to accomplish a social goal and to effect social transitions or spiritual transformations.[68] Randall Collins held that 'successful rituals created symbols of group membership and pumped up individuals with emotional energy'.[69] The nationalist government used symbols and rituals to serve the polity. The opening and closing ceremonies of the National Games were the main occasions for the use of these sensory rites and symbols: the involvement of the nationalist government, the attendance of politicians, speeches, banners, procession of athletes and representatives, and the national flags. The Games provided a stage on which to promote and reinforce Chinese nationalism because the arenas of these sports events were grand places that would normally attract hundreds of thousands of spectators.

For example, at the Fourth National Games in Hangzhou in 1930, Chiang Kai-shek, the leader of the nationalist party in Nanjing, together with his wife Soong Mei-ling and other politicians from the nationalist government, attended the opening ceremony. Chiang Kai-shek was also the honorary president of the Fourth National Games. He conducted these symbolic rituals, such as the raising of flags of the national state and the nationalist party; standing solemnly and silently in front of the photo of Sun Yat-sen for three minutes, and reading the political testament of Sun Yat-sen.[70] The nationalist government made full use of the impact of Sun Yat-sen to awaken the nation and to motivate them to fulfil his political ideal for national salvation.

Chiang Kai-shek gave his opening address at the ceremony of the Fourth National Games and stated that (see Figure 2.1):

> The National Games is a demonstration of the Chinese nation's resistance to imperialism; it also shows an independent spirit that the Chinese nation has a way to refuse all the warlords' reactionary forces. The National Games aim to complete the national revolution and the construction of the Three People's Principles in order to get rid of the Chinese national disgrace in modern history. . . . At the time of the invading of the imperialists from the outside and the civil wars among warlords inside China, I sincerely hope that all the people involved in the Games will promote the spirit of sport for national salvation and also strengthen the physique of our Chinese nation. Let's fight for the future of our motherland of China.[71]

Figure 2.1 President Chiang Kai-shek Addressing the Crowd at the Fourth National
Games in Republican China, 1933

Source: 'The Opening Ceremony of the Fourth National Games,' *Liangyou Huabao (良友画报)*,
no. 46 (1930): 3.

Later, Chiang Kai-shek met all of the athletes at the banquet, and he
required all athletes to perform well to show China's new spirit and to
take the responsibility of achieving Chinese national salvation through
sport.[72]

It had been planned to hold the Fifth National Games in 1931 in Nanjing.
However, due to two incidents in 1931 – the flood in Chang Jiang River and
the Mukden Incident (which led to Japan's occupation of three provinces in
Northeast China in 1931) – it was postponed to October 1933.[73] Wang Shijie (王世杰), the Minister of Education of the nationalist government, was
appointed as the President of this gathering. In his address at the opening
ceremony, he pronounced that:

> This is the second National Games under the nationalist government
> in Nanjing . . . our nationalist party's leader, Chiang Kai-shek, and the
> central government value the National Games because it is the best way
> to publicize the importance of sport. Sport can not only strengthen the
> nation's physique, but also enable people to form a military disciplin-
> ary. The British people always say that their politicians or their busi-
> nessmen are trained on the sports fields of their colleges. The biggest
> achievement of sport is not only a strong body but also a strong mind.[74]

The representative of the central nationalist party, Shao Yuanchong (邵元冲),
stated in his speech that 'the National Games is a practice of Sun Yat-sen's
political testament' and he acclaimed that 'only the one who both has a strong
body and mind could save the depraved Chinese nation'.[75]

Apart from these routine rituals of the Games, the most impressive ritual at the opening ceremony of the Sixth National Games was the procession of the athletes from the Northeast of China. While parading into the sports stadium, these athletes wore dark mourning dresses and flew the black and white flag, which was a symbol to remind the nation that the Northeast was under Japanese control after the Mukden Incident in 1931, but the Chinese should never forget that the land of the Northeast rightly belonged to them. The 10,000 spectators at the opening ceremony responded to the meaning of this symbol, and they shouted to express the shared hope of getting back the lost land. The rituals of the National Games utilized Chinese people as a national community to proclaim the territorial integrity and to revolt against the invasion of the Japanese.

Pierre Bourdieu has stated that 'the calendar is indeed one of the most codified aspects of social existence'.[76] The Fifth and Sixth National Games in 1933 and 1935 were both opened on 10 October when the National Day of the Republican China was celebrated. The significance of declaring the opening of the National Games on the same day as the National Day was twofold and was described in the report of *ShishiYuebao*:

> It helps us to memorize the great glory of former revolutionaries for the founding of the Republic China, to rethink how to be inspired and to shoulder the great responsibilities for this nation; it also helps us to see clearly the current situation that China faces.[77]

There were also ceremonies to celebrate the approaching National Day before the actual opening of the Fifth and the Sixth National Games. These ceremonies delivered messages of Chinese nationalism, such as 'Do not forget the shame of our nation on the National Day' or 'Abolish economic relationships with Japan forever'. Lin Sen (林森), the president of the nationalist government at the time, also underlined in his speech that 'It is essential to celebrate the National Day. We should never forget the national humiliation . . . let us be united and fight for our nation'.[78]

China was locked in the Second Sino-Japanese War from 1937 to 1945. The Seventh National Games in Shanghai were put on hold and suspended for more than 10 years until 1948. The nationalist government sponsored the Seventh National Games in order to reinforce national consciousness among its people and also to inspire the national spirit. It was the first time that a Taiwanese delegation (as representative of Taiwan Province) participated in the Games. Taiwan had been occupied by Japan after the first Sino-Japanese War in 1895, and had only recently been returned to China after the Second Sino-Japanese War. Chiang Kai-shek issued a written order for this meeting. The Organizing Committee decided to use the torch relay to deliver his order from Nanjing to Shanghai. This relay lasted for three days and was similar to today's Olympics torch relay. Eight teams carried the torch a distance of approximately 380 kilometres from Nanjing to Shanghai, and the runners were treated as national heroes. This new ritual attracted the public: many students gave flowers and silk banners as gifts to the runners, and some local governments organized people to run with them. Chiang Kai-shek's order was finally delivered to the Jiangwan Sports Stadium, where it was read at the opening ceremony by the general referee, Wang Zhengting.[79]

Politicization of the National Games under the Nanjing nationalist government

Benedict Anderson has claimed that the newspaper, as one of the most popular mass media, was a common symbol and a shared source across a very wide social network.[80] Members of the group's inter-connections with other groups were established across the entire political community.[81] In the process of nation-building in Republican China, the mass media became a shared resource in order to spread the political ideology of the central government and to publicize these National Games through the interactions of the nationalist government, the athletes and the general public. It can be illustrated from the following perspectives.

The propaganda mottos of the National Games and the carnival for the athletes in the period during the Games well illustrated the intimacy between sports events and politics. The sports arena itself was the best mass-media conduit for the promotion of Chinese nationalism because the intensity of the competitions at the arena attracted many spectators. Posters with propaganda mottos were also pasted around sports arenas. At the Fifth National Games, held in Nanjing Central Sports Stadium in 1933, these posters had messages such as 'Develop national sport, mobilize national spirit; only a sound nation could have a strong national state; Promote sport among all people to realize national salvation'.[82] A banner at the opening ceremony of the Sixth National Games in 1935 urged people to 'Develop sport to recover the national spirit; Promote sport to cultivate cooperation of the public'; 'Advocate sport to nourish Chinese nation's life'; 'A powerful country must have strong citizens and the salvation of a nation comes after self-improvement of its people'.[83] At the opening ceremonies of the Fourth, Fifth and Sixth National Games, hundreds of thousands of people – both audiences and athletes – were exposed to the messages and symbolism that espoused the cooperation between sport and national identity.[84] These rituals united the audience members and, with the help of the mass media, including newspapers and radio, a patriotic sentiment was delivered, which became a powerful source for the unification of the Chinese people.

The arrangement of the inductions and orientations for the athletes also provided a patriotic education to the nation. For instance, the Fifth National Games in 1933 took place approximately two years after the Mukden Incident of 18 September 1931. The first programme for the athletes was a screening of the documentary film about the Mukden Incident and the Japanese occupation of Shenyang in Northeast China. All of the athletes were touched by this film, and while viewing it they shouted 'Fight with the Japanese invaders' and 'Get back the lost land of the Northeast provinces'. They also sang the famous '18 September War Song'.[85] The theme of the song was to remind the Chinese nation of the loss of land to the Japanese imperialists and to fight for the sovereignty of the state. These interactions between the audience, the film and the song made the arena of the National Games a centre full of national sentiment and identity.

Some athletes and other non-governmental sports organizations openly displayed patriotic sentiment before, during and after the National Games. At the closing ceremony of the Fifth National Games in 1933, athletes from Japanese-occupied Northeast China delivered a farewell speech. The speech expressed their longing to reclaim the lost homeland. They insisted that the highest achievement of the National Games was not the sports accomplishments, but to show China as a unified force.[86] Three days later, athletes Shi Xinglong, Shi Xingwu, Shi Xinglu and Shi Ruisheng from Liaoning province in Northeast China, which was occupied by the Japanese, swam across the Yangtze River. They asked the journalists gathered there to report their patriotic actions, which they had undertaken for the purpose of awakening the nation to support the other 40 million Chinese people in Northeast China who were still ruled by the Japanese.[87] Lu Ju, a famous Chinese poet, created a poem entitled 'Ode to the Athletes',[88] which claimed that the real victory for the Chinese nation would occur on the day when China re-unified all the lost territories.[89] These actions demonstrated to the world that the Northeast was an inseparable part of China, and the Chinese people had a developed sense of national identity and a longing to live in an independent and sovereign nation-state.

The athletes from Northeast China played their part in bringing attention to their plight at the Fifth National Games in 1933. Many of these young athletes had escaped from Japanese occupation and had settled in other parts of China. At the opening ceremony, a delegation of these exiled athletes raised a banner while walking into the arena, which showed the four lost provinces in the Northeast. At the opening ceremony, representatives of the athletes took an oath to 'fight for the re-unification of China'.[90] Zhang Xinfu, a sports expert, stated that:

> our compatriot from the lost territories in Northeast China and also the overseas Chinese are all passionate in joining in the National Games,

which means that Chinese people, no matter where we are, are united for the defence of our motherland . . . it also tells the world that violence could only capture the land of our nation, but not our national spirit and the Chinese people's identity. We believe that someday we will reclaim the sovereignty of all the lost territories. The National Games today also has its contribution in uniting all Chinese people.[91]

At the opening ceremony of the Sixth National Games, athletes from Northeast China wore dark mourning and upheld the black and white flag (see Figure 2.2) as a reminder that Northeast China was still occupied by Japanese imperialists, and the land rightly belonged to China. The point was to arouse the Chinese audience members' patriotic sentiment to fight with the Japanese invaders. Their patriotic parade was echoed by thousands of Chinese compatriots with the help of the paper media.

In summary, years of wars in the Republican era resulted in punctuated performances in sport by Chinese athletes. However, the National Games

Figure 2.2 Black and White Flag at the Opening Ceremony of the Sixth National Games in Republican China, 1935

Source: 'Special for the Memory of the Sixth National Games: 200 photos,' *Painting Life (美术生活)*, no.20 (1935): 05.

demonstrated how China achieved its modernization of sport and how it reclaimed the sovereignty of sport from Westerners. The rituals and symbols of the National Games helped to simplify and amplify the national identity in particular circumstances. The nationalist government also carried its political ideology of national salvation into the National Games with the help of these shared resources.

The National Products Movement and the National Games

The National Products Movement (1900–1937) was a broad-based social movement that served to showcase the rapid development of Chinese nationalism during that era.[92] Karl Gerth has argued that 'the movement (as it was known at the time) created a nationalistic consumer culture that drove modern Chinese nation-making'.[93] By promoting the purchase of 'national products or Chinese-made products' as opposed to 'foreign products', the movement offered people of all classes an opportunity to resist imperialism and express their loyalty to the nation. This movement was not centrally controlled, but rather existed as an 'interactive set of institutions, discourses, and organizations which sought new ways to incorporate reluctant producers, merchants, and, above all, citizen-consumers'.[94] The movement emerged in the early 20th century as a reaction to the growing popularity of Western-inspired consumer goods. The movement sought to mobilize Chinese consumers in a commercial way in which their weapon was to buy only Chinese-made products. From 1905 and into the 1930s, boycotts of foreign goods also contributed to the movement's growth. This movement was also supported by the nationalist government. The Chinese National Product Exhibition in Shanghai in 1928 and the Chinese National Product Exhibition in Hangzhou in 1930, both of which were organized in conjunction with the nationalist government, joined the movement's import substitution ideology.[95] The Nanjing nationalist government designated 1933 as 'the National Products Year', 1934 as 'the Female National Products Year' and 1935 as 'the Student National Products Year'. The National Products Movement during this era was doomed to fail because of the backwardness of productivity in China, but to some degree it did stimulate the technical innovation of Chinese domestic production.[96]

The close ties between the National Games and the National Products Movement added a significant dimension to the development of Chinese nationalism in sport. As previously mentioned, the First National Games in 1910 were held on the grounds of the Nanyang Industrial Exposition in Nanjing. This exposition was a great celebration of the achievement of a capitalist economy, and the modern ethos of production, construction and consumption in China, and the First National Games seemed the perfect moment for such a public and spectacular breakthrough in Chinese national strength and unification.[97] In 1930 the Fourth National Games in Hangzhou was held at the same time as the Hangzhou West Lake Chinese National Product Exhibition; in 1935 the opening day of the Sixth National Games in Shanghai coincided with the Student National Products Year. Thereafter, the anti-Japanese war bolstered the relationship between the National Games and the National Products Movement when the sports arena of the Games began advertising Chinese-made products.

In line with this movement, sports products at the National Games were gradually replaced by national products rather than existing as imported commodities. At the beginning of the 20th century, sports products such as footballs, volleyballs, basketballs, different bats and sports shoes were predominantly imported from Japan, the United Kingdom, the United States, Germany and other European countries. Some foreign businessmen also began to sell sports products in large shopping malls and alien corporations in Fuli, Huiluo or Huisi in Tianjin and Shanghai.[98] After the Second National Games in 1914, some foreign businessmen in Shanghai and Kong Hong found sports products to be a lucrative commercial opportunity, and they expanded their stores and companies in China to sell a variety of sports goods, for instance, Shanghai Shengjihao and Shanghai Eastern Asia Company.[99]

The supply of imported sports equipment remained unchanged until the end of the 1920s when some patriotic Chinese industrialists began to produce sports products. There was an upsurge in the number of sports goods companies and factories in China in order to meet the growing demand for sports equipment in Chinese society. Buyun (布云) in Baoding, Hebei Province and Lisheng (利生) and Chuhe (春和) in Tianjin were examples of such companies.

Buyun in Baoding was initially a factory for the manufacture of music supplies that also offered some imported sports products for sale. From 1915, Buyun began to produce its own sports products, mainly footballs, basketballs, discus, javelins and racquets. With the expansion of production, Buyun became one of the most famous sports goods production corporations between 1926 and 1929. Buyun was very popular not only in the domestic market but also in Southeast Asia and some European countries, and was described as a company with 'perfect facilities, ingenious technicians and a wealth of experience'.[100] With the support of the Ministry of Education of the Nanjing government, Buyun represented China at the World Sports Products Exhibition, and its products won good reviews. Buyun made many efforts to promote its products to the general public in order to consolidate national self-strengthening and confidence. Its sports equipment was used as the appointed product for the North China Sports Games and the Fifth

National Games in 1933. Wang Shijie, the Minister of Education, wrote an inscription 'You Gong Tiyu (有功体育)' for the appreciation of Buyun's contributions to Chinese sport. With the help of the Games, Buyun also advertised in *QinfenTiyuYuebao*, a monthly sports magazine, to encourage more people to choose national products.[101] During the period of the anti-Japanese war, at the height of the boycott of Japanese products, Buyun relocated to Chongqing, in the southwest of China, increased its productivity and subsequently re-named itself as the Chinese Sports Products Company.

Another famous sports company was called Lisheng. Its founder was Sun Runsheng from Tianjin. In 1918, Sun began to make basketballs, footballs and volleyballs in Tianjin. He then founded Lisheng in 1920.[102] It became a relatively large company in the early 20th century, with more than 300 workers, 200 workshops and a variety of sports products. The factory was supervised by a leather technician who had been educated at Carleton University in the United States. The advanced technology and equipment from the United States were used to manufacture all kinds of leather products, which guaranteed the high quality of Lisheng's sports products.[103] The basketballs made by Lisheng were very popular and were appointed the official balls for the Fifth and Sixth National Games.[104] Lisheng's advertising slogan for its products was, 'The new and powerful sports equipment for the development of a strong Chinese nation'.[105]

Chunhe, another sports products manufacturer in Tianjin, was established in 1922. The founder of this company was Fu Bochuan, who was a friend of Zhang Boling, an influential educationalist of the Republican era. One day, Zhang Boling and Fu Bochuan discussed their worries about the backwardness of sport in China. Zhang mentioned that one of the factors that restricted the development of sport in China was the expense of imported sports products. This inspired Fu Bochuan to establish a domestic company to produce sports products.[106] Then, the three brothers, Fu Boquan, Fu Qinghuai and Fu Qingbo, established Chunhe and began to produce basketballs, footballs, tennis racquets and 20 other kinds of sports products. The lower-priced but quality products were favoured by Chinese athletes. In 1927, with increased production capacity and the large demand of the Chinese market, Chunhe not only produced various balls, but also sports shoes, equipment for track and field, and sportswear. In 1930 Fu Qinghuai studied in Europe and America for 10 months and visited an American sports goods company, Spalding, the largest sports goods company in the world at that time. He brought back more scientific management and advanced technology to Chunhe. In 1933 Chunhe's basketball was appointed as the ball for the Fifth National Games, and in 1935 the company's sports goods won great acclaim because they were examined and approved by the organizing committee of the Sixth National Games in line with the new regulations of the Games.[107]

In addition, with the rising tide of 'sport for national salvation' or 'national-products for national salvation', many sports products companies donated products for the National Games to voice patriotism among athletes from different parts of China. Thus, the demand for sports products of the National Games and the National Products Movement during the Games accelerated the establishment and development of these national sports goods companies and, to a certain extent, maintained the Chinese national interest as well as playing key roles in Chinese nation-building.

To summarize, the birth of the 1910 National Games in China was a useful instrument for the missionary institution (YMCA) to promote modern Western sport in China and eventually to engage with Chinese people to promote Christianity in China. To some extent, it was evidence of cultural imperialism of the West to impose Western culture and political ideology into Chinese society. Arguably, at its early stages, the National Games had nothing to do with Chinese nationalism or national identity, and it was just a typical example of cultural imperialism in China. However, the hosting of the National Games from 1910 to 1924 assisted in fostering in Chinese people the value of sportsmanship. It also witnessed Chinese people's gradual acceptance of modern Western sport.

In 1927, the nationalist government grasped the opportunity to utilize this national mega-sports event to promote its political ideology and to display the rise of modern China as a legitimate nation-state. The National Games was part of the preparation for international sports events, the FECG and the Berlin and London Olympic Games, to promote China's international image as a modern nation-state, and showcased the modernization of sport in China. The National Games had close ties with Chinese nationalism, both from the political and the economic dimensions, especially from the 1920s to the 1940s. It was shaped by Chinese anti-imperialist nationalism, which dominated modern Chinese history and was a powerful platform for the promotion of a sense of Chinese internal unity.

Thus, the National Games in the Republican era helped give the Chinese people the recognition of a national identity and a longing to live in an independent and sovereign nation-state. In a climate of foreign invasions, frequent civil wars, an unstable political environment and an economic downturn, the hosting of the National Games were regarded as a conscious effort to build a unified nation-state, and they helped Chinese people to develop a sense of national identity and a longing to live in an independent, sovereign nation-state. To summarize, the National Games in the Republican era in China played a role that was much more significant than that of a simple sports event: the Games assisted in shaping Chinese independent nationhood and national identity.

Notes

1 Bairner, *Sport, Nationalism, and Globalization*, 163–177.
2 McLenighan Valjean, *China: A History to 1949* (Chicago: Children's Press, 1983).
3 Immanuel C. Y. Hsu, *The Rise of Modern China* (New York: Oxford University Press, 1990), 123.
4 Yutang Lin, *The Spirit of Chinese Culture* (Shanghai: Shanghai Guofeng Bookstore Press, 1941), 45–48.
5 James P. Harrison, *Modern Chinese Nationalism* (New York: Hunter College of the City University of New York, 1969).
6 Lu and Fan, *Sport and Nationalism in China*, 9.
7 Chunli Li, *Social and Culture Changes in Modern China* (Hangzhou: Zhejiang People's Publishing House Press, 1999), 85.
8 Morris, *Marrow of the Nation*, 12.
9 Yihua Xu, *Shanghai St John's University (1879–1952)* (Shanghai: Shanghai People's Press, 2009), 11–14. St John's University was an Anglican university located in Shanghai, China. Before the Chinese Civil War, it was regarded as one of the most prestigious universities in Shanghai and China. The University was founded in 1879 as St John's College by William Jones Boone and Samuel Isaac Joseph Schereschewsky, Bishop of Shanghai, by combining two pre-existing Anglican colleges in Shanghai.
10 Hua Tan, ed., *Chinese Sport History* (Beijing: Higher Education Press, 2009), 181.
11 Howard G. Knuttgen, Ma Qiwei and Wu Zhongyuan, eds., *Sport in China* (Leeds: Human Kinetics Publishers, 1990), 14.
12 Changsheng Gu, *Missionary and Modern China* (Shanghai: Shanghai People's Press, 1991): 102–164.
13 Zhengping Tian, *Chinese Overseas Students and the Modernization of Education in China* (Guangzhou: Guangdong Education Press, 1996), 53.
14 Zheng Wang, *Never Forget National Humiliation: Historical Memory in Chinese Politics and Foreign Relations* (New York: Columbia University Press, 2012), 151.
15 Qingyi Bao, a Chinese royalist newspaper initially issued abroad in Japan in 1898 after the failure of the Hundred Days of Reform, which was established by Liang Qichao while he was exiled in Japan and named after a student movement of the Han Dynasty in ancient China.
16 Jujia Ou, 'A Proposal on the Relationship between Political Reform and China', *Qingyi Bao* (No. 27), Japan, October 15, 1899, 5.
17 Jean Chesneaux, Marianne Bastid and Marie-Claire Bergere, *China from the Opium Wars to the 1911 Revolution* (New York: Harvester Press, 1977).
18 Zhongshan Sun, *Three People's Principles* (Hunan: Yuelu Press, 2000), 69–92.
19 Hsu, *The Rise of Modern China*, 459.
20 Chinese Academy of Social Sciences, *Complete Works of Sun Yat-sen*, Volume. 4 (Beijing: China Book Company.1981), 18.
21 The May Fourth Movement was an anti-imperialist, cultural and political movement growing out of student demonstrations in Beijing on May 4, 1919, protesting the Chinese government's weak response to the Treaty of Versailles, especially the Shandong Problem. These demonstrations sparked national protests and marked the upsurge of Chinese nationalism, a shift towards political

éé

mobilization and away from cultural activities, and a move towards populist base rather than intellectual elite.

22 Tse-tung Chow, *The May Fourth Movement: Intellectual Revolution in Modern China* (Cambridge: Harvard University Press, 1960).
23 Yuanpei Cai, 'Opinions on New Education Policies', in Gao Shuping, ed., *Complete Works of Cai Yuanpei*, Volume. 2 (Beijing: Zhong Hua Book Company, 1984): 130.
24 Tao Xingzhi (1891–1946) was a renowned 20th-century Chinese educator and reformer. He studied at Teachers College, Columbia University and returned to China to champion progressive education.
25 Xingzhi Tao, *Tao Xingzhi Education Analects*, Volume. 1 (Beijing: Education Press, 1981), 8–9.
26 Brownell, *Training the Body for China*, 54.
27 Hong Fan and Tan Hua, 'Sport in China: Conflict between Tradition and Modernity 1840s to 1930s', *The International Journal of the History of Sport* no. 19 (2002): 189–212.
28 Exner was born in Austria and moved to America when he was 11. He joined the YMCA when he was 16, and he was a classmate and a roommate of James Naismith, the creator of basketball, when they studied at Springfield College. He was sent to China as a missionary in 1908, and he advocated sports such as basketball, volleyball and football. At the same time, he created 'the YMCA's sport expert's class' and built the sport stadium in Shanghai and organized the first National Games. He went back to America because of sickness and died in 1943.
29 Mingxin Tang, *The History of the Republic of China's Participation in the Olympic Games* (Taipei: Chinese Taipei Olympic Committee, 1999), 68.
30 M. J. Exner, 'Report of M.J. Exner, Physical Director, Shanghai', *Annual Reports of Foreign Secretaries of the International Committee, October 1, 1910 to September 30, 1911*, Shanghai Archives, 1911, 199.
31 Gengsheng Hao, *Hao Gengsheng's Memoirs* (Taipei: Biography Literature Press, 1969), 21.
32 Exner,. 'Report of M.J. Exner, Physical Director, Shanghai', 199.
33 Chengdu Sport History Research Institution, ed., *Historical Document on Sport History in Modern China* (Chengdu: Sichuan Education Press, 1986), 470–471.
34 'China Is Getting Athletic', *Association Men* (No. 36), March 1911, 243.
35 Mingxin Tang, *Chinese Olympic Journey in the Republic Era* (Taipei: Taipei International Olympic Committee, 1999), 68.
36 Frans De Wachter, 'Sport as Mirror on Modernity', *Journal of Social Philosophy* 32, no. 1 (2001): 90–98.
37 Chengdu Sport History Research Institution, ed., *Historical Document on Sport History in Modern China*, 471–472.
38 Zhengjie Cai, 'YMCA and the Development of Physical Education and Sport in Modern China (1895–1928)' (Master Thesis, Taibei Normal University, Taiwan, 1992), 95–98.
39 Shen Bao, 'No. 1 Special Issue on the National Games', *Shen Bao*, October 10, 1933.
40 Chinese Sport History Committee, *Chinese Modern Sport History* (Beijing: Beijing Sport College Press, 1989), 147.
41 Guoqi Xu, *Chinese and Americans: A Shared History* (Cambridge, MA: Harvard University Press, 2014), 238.

42 Anderson, *Imagined Communities*, vii.
43 King, 'Nationalism and Sport', 250.
44 Ibid., 249–259.
45 Anthony King, *The European Ritual* (Aldershot: Ashgate, 2003).
46 Allison, 'Sport and Nationalism', 344–355.
47 Ibid., 354.
48 Maurice Roche, 'Nations, Mega-Events and International Culture', in Gerard Delanty and Krishan Kumar, eds., *The Sage Handbook of Nations and Nationalism* (London and Thousand Oaks: Sage, 2006): 260–272.
49 Gengsheng Hao, 'History and Significance of the National Games', *Xin Zhonghua* 3, no. 19 (1935): 61–63.
50 Chinese Academy of Social Sciences, *Complete Works of Sun Yat-sen*, Volume. 4 (Beijing: China Book Company, 1981).
51 Yat-sen Sun, 'The Solution of China's Issue', in The Chinese Academy of Social Science, ed., *The Selected Works of Sun Yat-sen* (Beijing: People's Press, 1956): 56.
52 Yujun Lu and Liang Bo, 'The China National Athletic Union in the Republic of China', *Historical Archives (Lishi Dangan)* no. 4 (2001): 105–106.
53 Morris, *Marrow of the Nation*, 78.
54 Xiong Xiling (1870–1937), Premier of Republican China from 1913 to 1914. After he left politics, Xiong was involved in some education and charity institutions to help the unfortunates of Beijing and Shanghai and to help the refugees during the anti-Japanese war. After the fall of Shanghai, he went to Hong Kong, where he died in December 1937.
55 Zhang Boling (1876–1951) was the founder of Nankai University and the Nankai system of schools. Fairbank, John King, *The Great Chinese Revolution: 1800–1985* (New York: Harper & Row, 1986).
56 Tang, *The History of the Republic of China's Participation in the Olympic Games*, 81.
57 Shiming Luo, ed., *General History of Sport in China, 1840–1926* (Beijing: People's Sport Press, 2008), 311.
58 Jianlin Liao, 'A Research on the Third National Games in the Republic China', *Qiusuo (Seeker)*, no. 4 (2004): 234.
59 Morris, *Marrow of the Nation*, 80–81.
60 Ziqi Zhang, 'An Overview of the National Games', *XinZhonghua (New China)* 3, no. 19 (1935): 63.
61 Shiming Luo and Zhao Jianhua, eds., *Chinese Sport History*, Volume. 4 (1927–1949) (Beijing: People's Sport Press, 2008), 130–133.
62 Luo and Jianhua, eds., *Chinese Sports History*, 130–133.
63 Shen Bao, 'No.1 Special Issue on the Sixth National Games', *Shen Bao*, October 10, 1935.
64 'An Overview of the National Games', *Liangyou Huabao* no. 81 (1933): 16–18; 'The Precious News of the National Games', *Beiyang Huabao* 26, no. 1313 (1935): 2–4; 'The Special Issue for the Sixth National Games: 200 Pictures', *Meishu Shenghuo* no. 20 (1935): 1–27.
65 'The Rules of Holding the National Games', *Government Bulletin of the Ministry of Education* 7, no. 11–12 (1935): 15.
66 Si Xuan, 'Best Wishes to the National Games', *Zhongxuesheng (Journal of Middle School Students)* no. 199 (1948): 1–3.
67 Chen Jianning, 'The Seventh National Games in Shanghai in 1948', *Shanghai Archives* no. 6 (2001): 21–22.

68 John J. MacAloon, ed., *Rite, Drama, Festival, Spectacle: Rehearsals toward a Theory of Cultural Performance* (Philadelphia: Institute for the Study of Human Issues, 1984), 250.

69 Collins, *Interaction Ritual Chains*, 149–150.

70 Shen Bao, 'The Fourth National Games Began with an Opening Ceremony in Hangzhou', *Shen Bao*, April 2, 1930, 3.

71 Journalist, 'The Fourth National Games', *National Weekly News* 7, no. 14 (1930): 3–5.

72 Ibid., 5.

73 Zhang, 'An Overview of the National Games', 65.

74 Yi Zhong. 'Records of the Fifth National Games', *ZhongyangShishiZhoubao 2 (Weekly News of the Central Government)* no. 14 (1933): 21–25.

75 QiaowuYuebao, 'The General Situation of the National Games', *QiaowuYuebao (Monthly Newspaper for Chinese Abroad)* no. 1 (1933): 88.

76 Pierre Bourdieu, *Outline of a Theory of Practice*, Volume. 16 (Cambridge: Cambridge University Press, 1977), 97.

77 Jinwei Wang, 'The Organizing of the Fifth National Games and the Opening Ceremonies', *ShishiYuebao* 9, no. 6 (1933): 833.

78 Shen Bao, 'The Fifth National Games in Nanjing', *Shen Bao*, October 11, 1933, 7.

79 Chen, 'The Seventh National Games in Shanghai in 1948', 129.

80 Anderson, *Imagined Communities*, 32–33.

81 Ibid., 35.

82 Yi Zhong, 'Documentary of the Fifth National Games', *ZhongyangShishiZhoubao 2 (Weekly News of the Central Government)* no. 42 (1933): 4–9.

83 Nan, 'A Critical Review of the Sixth National Games', *ZhengzhiPinglun (Political Review)* no. 177 (1935): 743.

84 Shanghai Radio, 'Live Broadcast of the Seventh National Games', *GuangboZhoubao (Weekly Radio News)* no. 93 (1948): 12.

85 Editor, 'Reception and Recreation in the General Report of the Fifth National Games in the Republican China', Archives in Shanghai Library, Shanghai, 199.

86 Ju Lu, 'Ten Odes to the Fifth National Games', *People's Weekly* 2, no. 93 (1933): 12.

87 Sport Culture and History Archive, *Sport History Documents*, Volume. 6 (Beijing: People's Sport Press, 1981): 37.

88 The Ode on the Farewell for Athletes from the Northeast China in Chinese version, '一纸伤心告别书, 誰言血泪断肠词。河山破碎重整日，方是男儿得奖时。' It implied athletes' good wishes for the Chinese nation, and they considered the winning time to be when China regained all of the lost land.

89 Lu, 'Ten Odes to the Fifth National Games', 12.

90 Shen Bao, 'The Nationalist Government Held the Fifth National Games in Nanjing', *Shen Bao*, October 10, 1933, 9.

91 Xinfu Zhang, 'The Significance of the National Games', *ShishiYuebao* 9, no. 4 (1933): 260.

92 Karl Gerth, *China Made: Consumer Culture and the Creation of the Nation* (Cambridge, MA: Harvard University Asia Center, 2003), 6–9.

93 Ibid., 4.

94 Ibid., 6.

95 Andrea McElderry, 'China Made: Consumer Culture and the Creation of the Nation by Karl Gerth Cambridge MA: Harvard University Asia Center, 2003', *The Journal of Asian Studies* 63, no. 4 (2004): 1099–1101.

96 Zhaohong Qiao, 'Study on the 1935 Student National Products Movement', *Chinese Social Economic History Research* 4 (2007): 96–102.
97 Morris, *Marrow of the Nation*, 13.
98 Xianguo Li, 'Research on the Manufacture and Selling of Sports Products in the Early 20th Century', *Journal of Sport Culture Guide* no. 1 (2011): 40.
99 Xiaoqing Su and Jiandong Yi, 'Study on the Production and Marketing of Modern Chinese Sports Products', *Journal of Sport History* 3, no. 30 (1997): 1.
100 Institute of Sport History of Chengdu Sport University, *Reference of the Sport History in Modern China* (Chengdu: Sichuan Education Press, 1988): 225.
101 'The Special Issue of the Fifth National Games', *QinfenTiyuYuebao* 1, no. 11 (August 1934): 740.
102 Xiaoyang Zhao, 'Road to Masculinity: Contributions of YMCA on Modern Sport History in China', *Journal of Nanjing Sport University* 17, no. 2 (2003): 11–14.
103 Tianjin Sport Association, 'Lisheng Factory's Policy: High Quality, Good Service, Even Price, and Guaranteed', *Yearbook of Tianjin Sport Association* (1934): 23–26.
104 'General Report on the Fifth National Games', *QinfenTiyuYuebao* 1, no. 11 (1934): 8.
105 Luo and Zhao, eds., *Chinese Sport History*, 283.
106 Yishan Lu, 'History of Tianjin Chunhe Sports Products Manufacturer', *QinfenTiyuYuebao* 2, no. 1 (1934): 10–13.
107 Xianguo Li and Shan Huang, 'Study on the Development of Modern Sport Advertisement', *Journal of Sport Culture Guide* no. 8 (2011): 133–136.

References

Allison, Lincoln. 'Sport and Nationalism.' In *Handbook of Sports Studies*, edited by Jay Coakley and Eric Dunning, 344–355. London and Thousand Oaks: Sage, 2000.
Anderson, Benedict. *Imagined Communities: Reflections on the Origin and Spread of Nationalism*. London: Verso Books, 2006.
Bairner, Alan. *Sport, Nationalism, and Globalization: European and North American Perspective*. Albany: SUNY Press, 2001.
Bourdieu, Pierre. *Outline of a Theory of Practice*, Vol. 16. Cambridge: Cambridge University Press, 1977.
Brownell, Susan. *Training the Body for China: Sports in the Moral Order of the People's Republic*. Chicago: University of Chicago Press, 1995.
Chengdu Sport History Research Institution, ed. *Historical Document on Sport History in Modern China*. Chengdu: Sichuan Education Press, 1986.
Chinese Academy of Social Sciences. *Complete Works of Sun Yat-Sen*, Vol. 4. Beijing: China Book Company, 1981.
Chinese Sport History Committee. *Chinese Modern Sport History*. Beijing: Beijing Sport College Press, 1989.
Chow, Tse-tung. *The May Fourth Movement: Intellectual Revolution in Modern China*. Cambridge: Harvard University Press, 1960.
Collins, Randall. *Interaction Ritual Chains*. Princeton: Princeton University Press, 2004.
Gerth, Karl. *China Made: Consumer Culture and the Creation of the Nation*. Cambridge, MA: Harvard University Asia Center, 2003.

Gu, Changsheng. *Missionary and Modern China*. Shanghai: Shanghai People's Press, 1991.

Hao, Gengsheng. *Hao Gengsheng's Memoirs*. Taipei: Biography Literature Press, 1969.

Hao, Gengsheng. 'History and Significance of the National Games.' *Xin Zhonghua* 3, no. 19 (1935): 61–63.

Harrison, James P. *Modern Chinese Nationalism*. New York: Hunter College of the City University of New York, 1969.

Hsu, Immanuel C. Y. *The Rise of Modern China*. New York: Oxford University Press, 1990.

King, Anthony. 'Nationalism and Sport.' In *The Sage Handbook of Nations and Nationalism*, edited by Gerard Delanty and Krishan Kumar, 249–259. Thousand Oaks: Sage, 2006.

King, Anthony. *The European Ritual*. Aldershot: Ashgate, 2003.

Li, Chunli. *Social and Culture Changes in Modern China*. Hangzhou: Zhejiang People's Publishing House Press, 1999.

Liao, Jianlin. 'A Research on the Third National Games in the Republic China.' *Qiusuo (Seeker)* no. 4 (2004): 234.

Lin, Yutang. *The Spirit of Chinese Culture*. Shanghai: Shanghai Guofeng Bookstore Press, 1941.

Lu, Zhouxiang, and Fan Hong. *Sport and Nationalism in China*. London and New York: Routledge, 2013.

Luo, Shiming, ed. *General History of Sport in China, 1840–1926*. Beijing: People's Sport Press, 2008.

Luo, Shiming, and Zhao Jianhua, eds. *Chinese Sport History*, Vol. 4 (1927–1949). Beijing: People's Sport Press, 2008.

MacAloon, John J., ed. *Rite, Drama, Festival, Spectacle: Rehearsals toward a Theory of Cultural Performance*. Philadelphia: Institute for the Study of Human Issues, 1984.

Maurice, Roche. 'Nations, Mega-vents and International Culture.' In *The Sage Handbook of Nations and Nationalism*, edited by Gerard Delanty and Krishan Kumar, 260–272. Thousand Oaks: Sage, 2006.

Morris, Andrew D. *Marrow of the Nation: A History of Sport and Physical Culture in Republican China*. Berkeley and Los Angeles: University of California Press, 2004.

Sun, Zhongshan. *Three People's Principles*. Hunan: Yuelu Press, 2000.

Tan, Hua, ed. *Chinese Sport History*. Beijing: Higher Education Press, 2009.

Tang, Mingxin. *The History of the Republic of China's Participation in the Olympic Games*. Taipei: Chinese Taipei Olympic Committee, 1999.

Tao, Xingzhi. *Tao Xingzhi Education Analects*, Vol. 1. Beijing: Education Press, 1981.

Tian, Zhengping. *Chinese Overseas Students and the Modernization of Education in China*. Guangzhou: Guangdong Education Press, 1996.

Valjean, McLenighan. *China: A History to 1949*. Chicago: Children's Press, 1983.

Wang, Zheng. *Never Forget National Humiliation: Historical Memory in Chinese Politics and Foreign Relations*. New York: Columbia University Press, 2012.

Xu, Guoqi. *Chinese and Americans: A Shared History*. Cambridge, MA: Harvard University Press, 2014.

3 Governance of sport and the National Games in the PRC, 1949–1979

The formation of China's sports policy and governance in the PRC

On 1 October 1949, at the founding moment of the People's Republic of China (PRC), Mao Zedong proclaimed to the world that 'ours will no longer be a nation subject to insult and humiliation. We have stood up'.[1] In Mao Zedong's eye, China's pre-liberation sufferings (before 1949) were as a direct result of the feudalism of the Qing Dynasty and the external Western imperialism.[2] Chinese nationalism, which was shaped by anti-feudalism and anti-imperialism, went side by side with Marxist ideology during the construction period of the new regime in order to win recognition from its people and outside of China and also to testify to the legitimacy of the PRC in this period.[3] Chinese nationalism was particularly hostile to the United States and Japan because the United States generally represented Western values, and Japanese imperialists had left the Chinese people with humiliation and injustices during World War II.[4] The Chinese government strove to make China completely independent via economic self-reliance. This perspective of nationalism was regarded as nativist nationalism, which kept China locked in poverty and economic backwardness in Mao Zedong's era.[5] In addition, the Chinese Communist Party (CCP) leadership was selective in their thinking towards the Chinese traditional culture; they acknowledged some elements but attacked most of China's traditional culture as feudal legacies.[6] This developed into a comprehensive anti-traditionalism during the Cultural Revolution (1966–1976). It was well illustrated by the Red Guard's destroying of the Four Olds[7] and the remnants of Confucianism within the 10 years of chaos of revolution.

It did not take long for the Chinese government to realize the significant political implication that sport could have in relation to the new PRC's national defence, the construction of a socialist society as well as its international image. Sport and athletes in this period were still endowed with a nationalist mission to transform the 'sick man of East Asia' into a strong and modern nation respected by the world.[8] China rushed holding the First National Congress of Sport and Physical Education in Beijing on 26–27 October 1949. It was chaired by Fen Wenbing, the secretary-General of the Chinese Communist Youth League (CCYL). He stated that sport in the PRC was utilized to serve 'people's health, new democratic construction and national defence'.[9] In 1952, Chairman Mao Zedong's inscription for the sole sport magazine at the time, *Xin Tiyu*, 'Develop sport and strengthen people's physique', became a favourable proverb in this period and contributed to the establishment of the important role of sport in people's lives. It indicates that the focus of Chinese sports policy was on mass sport and military sport to build healthy citizens for national defence in the early years of the PRC.

Besides, the Chinese government in Beijing had to reconstruct its sporting governing body since the previous one in the Republican era was transferred to Taiwan by the Nationalist Party. Drawing on experiences from the Soviet Union, a new Chinese sports governance system was run by the state government (the State Council), which reflected the wide socialist system in China, 'both the Party and state administrations were organized in a vast hierarchy with power flowing down from the top'.[10] On 15 November 1952, the central government established a national governing body of sport: the State Sport Ministry (SSM) in Beijing. Meanwhile, a non-governmental, non-profit sports organization at the national level, the All-China Sports Federation (ACSF), was established, which provided an important linkage between the Chinese government and the populace who were involved in sport. The ACSF functioned as the Chinese Olympic Committee[11] and was acknowledged by the International Olympic Committee (IOC) in 1954 as an official member.[12] However, due to the 'two Chinas' issue, the ACSF ceased its relationship with the IOC in 1958 until the IOC officially recognized the Chinese Olympic Committee as the representative body for China in 1979.

The Chinese government released 'Ten-year guidelines for sports development', which was seriously affected by the Great Leap Forward in late 1958.[13] This sports policy aimed to rapidly catch up with worldwide standards in both elite sport and mass sport within a decade.[14] Following the announcement of the radical Great Leap Forward, these 10-year sports guidelines called for some impossibly high targets for elite sport in 1958, such as to 'cultivate 50–70 million active athletes and 10–15 thousand elite athletes within ten years'.[15] In order to achieve these grandiloquent targets, many workers and peasants had to be trained intensively day and night via heavy physical exercises. On the contrary, it was not beneficial to their health.

This impractical sports policy was accordingly ceased in the early 1960s when the Chinese government realized the errors of the Great Leap

Forward. In sport, the focus shifted from developing both mass sport and elite sport at the same time to putting more emphasis on elite sport. For example, some new slogans for elite sports training principle were popularized to guarantee the development of Chinese elite sport since 1964, such as 'Three requirements and one heavy load',[16] 'Shorten the training period and give priority to develop some sports events', as well as 'Training and practising in domestic meets for better results in international sports stages'. In this period, Chinese sport made its progress under a relatively stable environment.

However, after Chairman Mao Zedong launched the Cultural Revolution in 1966,[17] it caused a serious damage to Chinese sports system in its early stages: the SSM and local sports committees were suspended their administrations and general affairs; many sports officials were denounced and humiliated by the Red Guards because elite sport was regarded as a bourgeois reactionary line. As Fan Hong stated, 'Competitive sports was damaged, the training system was dismantled, sports schools closed, sports competitions ceased, Chinese teams stopped going abroad and outstanding athletes were condemned as sons and daughters of the bourgeoisie and suffered mentally and physically'.[18] However, sport in the late period of the Cultural Revolution managed to survive under very complex and unique social, cultural and political circumstances, and it even managed to develop.[19] In 1971 China announced a widely known sports proverb, 'Friendship first, competition second' and sent its sport delegation to participate in the 31st World Table Tennis Championship in Japan in 1971. Zhuang Zedong's chance meeting with American table tennis player Glenn Cowan initiated Ping-Pong Diplomacy and triggered the first thawing of ice in Sino-American relations since 1949.[20]

After the Ping-Pong Diplomacy, Chinese athletes were encouraged to participate in international sports events as well as to visit other countries. China also positively staged some international sports events. For example, on 2 November 1971, the Asian-Africa Table Tennis Friendship Championship was staged in Beijing, which attracted athletes from 58 Table Tennis Associations as well as sports organizations from 49 countries or regions. This was the first time China staged an international sports event since the beginning of the Cultural Revolution. From 1972 to 1979, China organized many sports events within China at different levels and also had more involvement in sports events at the international level, such as the Seventh Asia Games in Teheran in 1974, the 1977 Summer Universidade, as well as the Eighth Asia Games in Bangkok in 1978. The Chinese nation was inspired and encouraged by Chinese athletes breaking up Asian records and world records in world sports arenas. Sport acted as a bridge and had proved extremely valuable for diplomacy in China.

The process of formation of sports policy in China reflects and contributes to changing political and diplomatic demands of the Chinese nation after the establishment of the PRC in 1949. In general, the period from 1949 to 1979 witnessed changing sports policy from the promotion of mass sport for socialist labour production and national defence, to more emphasis on elite sport to improve international prestige and enhance Chinese national unity. In this context, the National Games was restored and promoted.

The restoration of the National Games in 1959

The plan to host a National Games in the PRC was first officially proposed by Deng Xiaoping's five pieces of instructions to Rong Gaotang in reply to Gaotang's report on the Chinese delegation's visit to the Soviet Union in 1952. The visit took place when Gaotang and the delegation were returning from the Helsinki Olympic Games. Deng's five instructions were:

1   To begin to prepare the structure of the new ministry of sport;
2   To begin to recruit professional full-time athletes from the army and society;
3   To start to build an athletic stadium;
4   To begin to establish specialized sport institutions;
5   To host a National Games next year (1953).[21]

The Chinese government hoped to follow in the footsteps of the Soviet Union to become a sporting power by hosting national sports events. Due to China's economic backwardness in the early 1950s, Deng Xiaoping's instruction 'to hold a National Games next year (1953)' was not put into practice, yet it was the first time to put the hosting of the National Games on the agenda officially by the new Chinese government.[22]

The plan to host the National Games was conceived in 1956 when China released 'the Competitive Sport System of the PRC'. In 1958 the SSM proposed to the State Council that more competitive sports should be practiced in order to achieve an international level of sports performance. The Chinese government agreed with the SSM's suggestion and emphasized that sport could revive the national spirit. To demonstrate the achievement of the new China, the hosting of the First National Games in 1959 were incorporated into broad commemorations of the 10th anniversary of the PRC.[23] From its earliest iterations, the PRC's National Day (1 October) has been an expression and celebration of the way of life that emerged and continued to emerge in what is now the nation-state of China. The day is an explicit celebration of the represented values, traditions and beliefs of China. The National Games were projected as a programme to celebrate

the Chinese National Day. The central government explained the significance of the games:

> The National Games in this year is the first time since the establishment
> of the PRC in 1949 and it should be held successfully. It will be a tribute
> to celebrate the 10th anniversary of the country; it will facilitate the
> development of sport and create more new records in several competi-
> tive sports events with the collective intelligence. It is important to focus
> on some sports events that Chinese athletes are good at, to pay more
> attention to unity of all athletes, and to avoid encouragement of champi-
> onships and sporting heroes. It has great diplomatic significance.[24]

The managerial structures of the National Games in the PRC

Apart from celebrating the 10th anniversary of the PRC, the principles and
purposes of the First National Games in 1959 were clearly demonstrated in
its official slogans, including 'Build up the physical strength and serve Chinese industry and agriculture' and 'Exercise the body and protect the great
socialist mother country'.

The hosting of the Second National Games in 1965 cannot be separated
from the Games of the New Emerging Forces (GANEFO) because it aimed
to prepare Chinese athletes to attend the GANEFO. After the split with the
IOC and other international sporting federations in 1958, the CCP offered
an olive branch to the socialist countries in Asia, Africa and Latin America.
The first GANEFO was initiated by Indonesia in 1963 by leaders of the
Non-Aligned Movement as a counter to the IOC and the Fédération Interna-
tionale de Football Association (FIFA).[25] China was one of the GANEFO's
main supporters and sponsors. The purpose of the GANEFO was to 'develop
a community of nations . . . which ensures respect for each other's national
identity and national sovereignty'.[26] The GANEFO was a representative
case to show the politicization of sport.[27] It was regarded as a challenge
by the Third World nations to the Western hegemony of sport and demonstrated 'the political ambitions of the new and non-aligned states'.[28] China
and 35 other countries were declared as members of the GANEFO after
attending the first GANEFO in 1963. The second GANEFO was planned
to be held in 1967 in Cairo. Yet, the diplomatic relationship between China
and Indonesia ended in 1965. Cairo subsequently announced it could not
financially afford to host the second GANEFO, yet China could not support
it as China was in chaos from the Cultural Revolution. After the loss of the
prominent supporters, Indonesia and China, the GANEFO was ceased in
1966. This did not affect the hosting of China's Second National Games

in 1965 as scheduled, though it was designed to prepare Chinese athletes to succeed at the 1967 GANEFO. Additionally, China's Second Games in 1965 was also regarded as a sport gala to review 16 years of sport development in the early PRC from 1949 to 1965.[29]

The SSM highlighted that the Second National Games in 1965 would 'facilitate the development of mass sport, improve talented young athletes' performances in order to enhance China's international status and political power by achieving success at the GANEFO and other international sports competitions'.[30] The mottos of the Second National Games included 'Exercise the body, build our motherland and defend the nation'; 'Have the whole country in mind and the whole world in view'; and 'Marching forward courageously while upholding the great Mao Zedong's thought'.[31] These mottos were printed as the posters or on newspapers, or broadcasted via radio to publicize the games.

The Third National Games was held in Beijing in 1975, ten years after the Second Games in 1965. The purpose of the Third National Games was influenced by the Cultural Revolution and Chairman Mao's Marxist socialism. The Cultural Revolution was a movement with the 'mixture of both nativist anti-Western xenophobia and anti-traditionalist sentiment'.[32] The purpose was twofold by its motto, 'For the proletariat politics, for the proletarian'. It was also exemplified by one of the posters of the Third National Games.

On the poster (see Figure 3.1), an athlete is reading the book, *Marx, Engels, Lenin: On the Dictatorship of the Proletariat*. The background

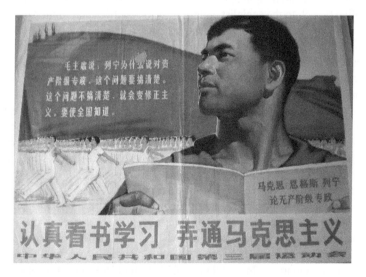

Figure 3.1 A Poster for the Third National Games in the PRC, 1975
Source: The GASC, 2006, p. 21.

of the poster is the red flag (the symbol of communism) and the athletes' parade. Mao's words were printed on the flag, 'It should be known nationally the reason why Lenin stated that we should realize the dictatorship of the proletariat over the bourgeoisie. This question should be clarified; otherwise, it will be revisionism'. The motto was on the bottom of the poster, 'Reading and upholding genuine Marxist theory'.[33] This poster was one of several representations that propagandized the Chinese government ideological orthodoxy of socialism and communism. It was a sensible way to disseminate the games as well as political ideologies to the general public in China.

The infancy year of Deng Xiaoping's reform and opening-up policy in China was 1979. Deng Xiaoping's policy was to defend and to seek China's national interests, which was also an infancy period of pragmatic nationalism, a national interest-driven goal that would focus on economic construction and 'Four Modernizations'.[34] The Fourth National Games was chosen to be held in 1979 to encourage the Chinese people after the 10 years of confusion of the Cultural Revolution. The principle of the Fourth National Games was illustrated by its promotional motto: 'Emancipating the mind and serving the modernization of the nation'. The Fourth National Games in 1979 was also utilized to celebrate the 30th anniversary of the PRC.[35]

It is clear that the principles and purposes of the first four National Games in the early PRC were in response to Chairman Mao Zedong's sports instruction, 'Develop sport and strengthen people's physique'. On the one hand, the hosting of the National Games aimed symbolically to overcome China's political and geographical division by legislating national unity, because the games assembled athletes from different regions in China to compete in a fair and impartial sports arena. On the other hand, it could be perceived as an opportunity to create a positive condition for the Chinese government to promote state ideologies and to demonstrate China's new image to its people. The aspiration of each games was guided by this general principle, but it had its own more specific objectives in different social historical contexts. No matter whether it was a project for celebrating the anniversary of the PRC, or a preparation for attending the GANEFO, or to inspire the Chinese people's sense of national identity, these games were shaped by Chinese politics and served its political requirement from the Chinese government.

In this period, the National Games was governed directly by the SSM under the State Council. The Ministry of Finance of the State had been committed to contributing financially to the staging of the National Games. Accordingly, the National Games became one of the state-led events in this new communist regime. The organization of the National Games was entrusted by the SSM to the local sport commission of the host province or municipality. In order to coordinate with every project of the National Games, a High Commission of the Preparatory Committee and Organizing Committee was established before each of the games. The Organizing Committee normally consisted of several sub-committees. Most members of the committee were officials and sport experts from the SSM and the CCYL, which showed that the Chinese government put considerable weight behind these National Games by providing leadership, human resources and financial funding.

The city, particularly the national or regional capital, is a landscape that embodies public memory, monuments, statuary or street names. These, in turn, become the stage for national and regional spectacle, parades and performance, which correspond to the sense of belonging to a nation or region.[36] The capital city Beijing was chosen as the site to host the first four National Games. This was because Beijing was a centre for both Chinese politics and economy in the early period of the PRC. Beijing was also chosen because the city's past validated the present, and created an unbroken cultural tie or a shared memory and myth. In contemporary times, it was thought that hosting the National Games in Beijing would allow competitors and spectators to draw on this recognized cultural and mythical past, and to transfer these feelings of reimagined pride and passion to the Chinese nation.

In order to stage the games, sports facilities and sports venues were required. Thus, the central government provided financial resources to build the Beijing Worker's Stadium (BWS). The BWS was one of the 10 buildings in Beijing to celebrate the 10th anniversary of the PRC in 1959 as well. Apart from the BWS, another nine buildings were constructed in Beijing, including the Great Hall of People, Museum of Chinese Revolution and History, China Military Museum, Beijing Train Station, National Agricultural Exhibition Center, Diaoyutai State Guesthouse, Beijing Cultural Palace of Nationalities, Beijing Minzu Hotel and the Beijing Prime Hotel. Along with these other nine buildings, the BWS became a symbol of the new PRC.

In order to prepare for these national sports events, many provinces or municipalities began to organize local sports events to select potential athletes and establish provincial sports teams to train athletes for the National Games. By the 1970s, every province in China had established its own professional sport teams, along with its own governing body sport, the Provincial Sport Commission, which was directed by the SSM.[37] In order to have a successful performance at the National Games, sports competitions at different levels were termly held.

The People's Liberation Army (PLA), the military system of China, also selected its athletes and organized its sports delegation to compete with other sports delegations at the provincial level. Throughout this period, China faced the Korean War, the Sino-India conflict, the Sino-Soviet split, the Vietnam War and the Taiwan issue, all of which linked sport with militarism in China.[38] Therefore, PLA's toughness, bravery and sacrifice in battle shaped the ideals of training in sport, as the training was also considered important to improve national defence power to maintain national security. In order to maintain the development of a lasting national defence, the SSM introduced the training philosophy from the PLA to local youth sports schools. The intention was to militarize Chinese athletes and to improve the sports performance of Chinese athletes.

Sports events at the National Games varied at each meet in this period, yet they included most of the major modern Western sports events and some of the military sports events. Military sports events, however, were programmed as competition or demonstration sports in these games. It is clear that the choice of sports events at the games reflects not only what sport the Chinese public played at the time, but also how sport fit in with the communist leaders' view of China's place in the world.

A diligently organized Taiwan province delegation by the Chinese government

Henry Kissinger said that, 'Whatever the cost, China will fight rather than give up what it considers Chinese territory'.[39] Taiwan's reunification concerns the most fundamental of China's vital national interests and Chinese national feeling, and it is 'a principal issue of national unity, sovereignty and territorial integration of China'.[40] Taiwan is a typical example of Chinese humiliation because it was invaded and bullied by Western imperialist countries and Japan in history. For its legitimacy and authority, the Chinese government treated Taiwan as a local province belonging to the PRC and framed its determination to 'liberate' Taiwan from the control of Chiang Kai-shek and his Nationalist Party.[41] In addition, Taiwan had its geostrategic significance as a bulwark against imperialists, the United States and Japan.[42] In the PRC's early years, the CCP conducted many favourable proposals for the aims of the Chinese nation's unification, and among them 'liberation of Taiwan' was regarded as one of the manifestations of the 'one China principle' for national security and territorial integrity.[43]

Accordingly, sport became a useful vehicle to make the new Chinese government's standpoint towards Taiwan.[44] With permission of the Chinese government, the SSM and the Organizing Committee of the Third and Fourth Games in 1975 and 1979 tactically organized a Taiwan province delegation to compete at the National Games. However, the Taiwan province delegation was made up of Taiwanese compatriots who resided in mainland China, Hong Kong, Macao and overseas, rather than athletes chosen by the Nationalist government in Taiwan. The Chinese government seized the opportunity to publicize Taiwan as being part of China for the past 1,000 years and to show that Taiwan's division from China was temporary.

With support of the Chinese government, a founding meeting of the Taiwan province delegation for the Third National Games was held in the Beijing Hotel on 23 August 1975. About 500 people attended the inaugural meeting, including officials from the SSM, PLA and Organizing Committee of the Third National Games, members of the National People's Congress (NPC) and the Chinese People's Political Consultative Conference (CPPCC), along with 279 athletes and representatives in the Taiwan province delegation.[45] Cai Xiao, the head of the Taiwan province delegation, represented the Taiwanese compatriots to address:

> the establishment of Taiwan province delegation declared Chairman Mao Zedong and the Chinese government's concern about 16,000,000 Chinese people in Taiwan . . . the involvement of Taiwanese athletes at the National Games indicates that Taiwanese are blood compatriots of the big family of Chinese nation of all ethnic groups and Taiwan is an inalienable part of the inviolable territory of China. We believe that these sporting competitions and all kind of activities during the games will enhance the kindred feelings between our compatriots in Taiwan and the mainland and will play a positive role in the socialist revolution as well as sport development in the motherland. . . . We firmly believe that with the rising patriotic sentiment among our compatriots in Taiwan and mainland, the reunification of our motherland will be realized soon.[46]

In the 1970s the budget for the National Games from the Chinese government was restricted by its weak economic situation. The Organizing Committees of the Third and Fourth National Games provided the renowned Beijing Youyi Hotel (one of the best hotels in Beijing at the time) for the Taiwan delegations, but hostels were provided for most of the athletes from other provinces or autonomies within China. Moreover, the hotel provided special Taiwanese food for these athletes to help them perform better at the National Games.[47]

At the opening ceremonies of the Third and Fourth Games, when the Taiwanese athletes entered the stadium, people welcomed them with warm applause. Both inside and outside the sports arena, athletes from Taiwan and mainland China shared the joy of reunification. *A Story of Pomelos* at the Third National Games illustrated the flesh-and-bone compatriotism between athletes in the mainland and Taiwan by the Chinese media.[48] Pomelo was introduced to the Sichuan province in the 18th century from Taiwan. It was reported that at the basketball court of the Third National Games, athletes from Sichuan province shared pomelos with athletes from Taiwan province after competition. A basketball player from the Taiwan province delegation was touched by this warm scene and wrote a poem to express his joy at being back in the motherland and to share his good wishes for the reunification of Taiwan and the mainland.[49]

It was clear that the formation of the Taiwan province delegation by the Chinese government at the Third and Fourth National Games was intertwined with China's politics. By doing so, the state leaders in China made their stance clear to the nation and world in the sports arena, stating their quest for national sovereignty over Taiwan to maintain territorial integrity of the Chinese nation.

Since the early 1980s, the new communist leadership in China stopped using the rhetoric of 'Liberating Taiwan', emphasizing instead a peaceful reunification through negotiation, a more mildly rhetorical and pragmatic notion.[50] The nationalist sport authorities in Taiwan, however, did not send any sports delegations to attend the National Games in mainland China because this might imply that Taiwan is an administrative province under the PRC government, which Beijing had been insisting and Taipei had been resisting till now. The Chinese government in Beijing also ceased organizing a sport delegation to represent Taiwan to attend the National Games for the purpose of figurative or symbolic reunification of China.

One of the respondents, a sports expert in Taiwan, claimed that

> the Taiwan authorities did not send athletes to attend the National Games, but Taiwan was a democratic society which allowed its citizens to participate in any sports events in their own names (not in the name of the Taiwanese government). Maybe Taiwanese athletes would participate in future National sports events with an unofficial name and a low-pitched attitude.[51]

Hence, the Taiwan province delegation at the Third and Fourth National Games in the 1970s was dedicatedly utilized by the Chinese government under the CCP's leadership as propaganda to highlight its desire for sovereignty over Taiwan. It puts the CCP regime's official discourse of national identity in Mao Zedong's era directly in the spotlight of the National Games.

Symbolic capital of the National Games in the PRC

The format of the National Games in the PRC was derived from both the Soviet model and the Olympic Games.[52] Apart from sports competitions, the cultural symbols and rituals, opening and closing ceremonies, delegations parades, mass calisthenics, and torch relays derived from the CCP and were orchestrated to express the symbolism of the Chinese nation to the Chinese people.[53]

Cultural symbols, such as the national flag and/or emblem, national anthem and currency, are crucial to the construction of a nation. They constitute collective memories among large segments of the population.[54] Chairman Mao Zedong considered the cultural symbols to be 'powerful weapons for uniting and educating the people and for attacking and destroying the enemy'.[55] Before each of the National Games, the Organizing Committee would design and release several cultural symbols as publicity. These designed semiotic devices included an emblem, National Games' flag with the image of the emblem, anthem, posters, pamphlets, torch, commemorative stamps, medals, cups and so forth. The representative symbol of the first four National Games was made up of the emblems, posters, commemorative stamps, attendance of the state leadership and their delivered speeches (see Figure 3.2). For example, the emblem of the Fourth National Games contained a red flaming torch and a golden racetrack, which symbolized a new era of political and economic reform after the ending of Mao Zedong's tumultuous Cultural Revolution.

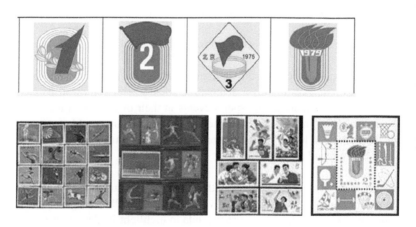

Figure 3.2 Emblems and Commemorative Stamps of the First, Second, Third and Fourth National Games in the PRC

Source: The GASC, 2006, pp. 23–75.

Despite emblems of the National Games, there was a torch relay entitled, 'The 25,000-Li New Long March Torch Relay' at the Fourth Games.[56] The torch relay began on 1 July 1979 in Shanghai, the birthplace on the birthday of the CCP. The vice-premier Wang Zhen lit the torch for the relay. The 77 days of the 25,000-Li New Long March Torch Relay travelled through 16 cities and reached some of the CCP's memorial sites of the war of liberation.[57] The torch relay attracted many spectators.[58] The relay publicized the National Games and mobilized the general public's enthusiasm towards sport; more importantly, by incorporating revolutionary history of the CCP into the torch relay, the younger generation gained a sense of continuity with the CCP history and could appreciate China's political and social progress. At the same time, the torch relay symbolized that China, which was led by the CCP, would march into modernization in a new era. After the Fourth National Games in 1979, torch relay became a routine programme for the following future National Games.

In order to promote the National Games, the Organizing Committee also issued posters for each of the games. Many posters also indicated China's political ideologies at the time. For example, in the turbulent decade of the Cultural Revolution, the Organizing Committee of the Third National Games issued a series of posters that were then printed in a large number for distributing nationwide. The mottos and images of these posters exemplified many aspects of Mao Zedong's ideological orthodoxy of the revolutionary spirit of peasants, workers, and soldiers to ensure the national unity and economic prosperity. These posters were replete with iconography of peasants, workers, and soldiers. Some examples are: 'Serve the proletarian revolution, Serve the peasants, workers, and soldiers' (see Figure 3.3), 'Bombard the capitalist headquarters', 'Reading and learning the Marxist, Leninist, and Mao Zedong Thought', 'Thoroughly revolutionize the battlefronts of ideas and culture' and 'Develop sport and strengthen people's physique' (see Figure 3.3). Many posters also illustrated the patriotic and nationalistic sentiments, which were entitled as follows: 'Chinese people have the ambitions and are capable of catching up and exceeding the production of the USA and UK soon', 'Red Flower turn to the Sun, bless our great motherland forever' as well as 'Athletes from all ethnic groups march forward to a bright future corporately'.

In addition, these four National Games closed just before or overlapped with the PRC National Day on 1 October (see Table 3.1). The number of people in Beijing was twofold because of celebrations of the National Day. The spectators of these Games included the state leaders of the central government, members from the SSM, athletes, coaches, invited foreign guests and thousands of audiences from schools, offices and factories. They all witnessed and were inspired by the success of sports development as well as the new image of China.

Figure 3.3 Poster for the Third National Games in the PRC, 1975
Source: The GASC, 2006, pp. 57–58.

The attendance of state leaders (see Table 3.1) signified the Chinese government's support for the games. For instance, Chairman Mao and Premier Zhou Enlai attended the First and Second National Games;[59] President Hua Guofeng attended the Fourth Games; and Deng Xiaoping was present at all of the opening ceremonies of the first four Games.

The ceremonies and competitions attracted thousands of people from all walks of life as well as athletes of different delegations from all over China and also many students in Beijing.[60] Chairman Mao, as a uniting figure, attended the opening ceremony of the First and Second National Games, which inspired many people, especially the young. This was also the best way for Chairman Mao to propagandize state ideologies to his populace.

Table 3.1 Attendance of State Leaders at the Opening and Closing Ceremonies, 1959–1979[61]

Edition and Time	The Opening Ceremony	The Closing Ceremony
1. 13 September to 3 October 1959	Mao Zedong, Liu Shaoqi, Zhou Enlai, Zhu De, Deng Xiaoping, Dong Biwu, etc.	Liu Shaoqi, Zhou Enlai, Zhu De, Deng Xiaoping, Peng Zhen, Chen Yi, Li Fuchun, etc.
2. 11–28 September 1965	Mao Zedong, Liu Shaoqi, Zhou Enlai, Zhu De, Deng Xiaoping, Dong Biwu, etc.	Liu Shaoqi, Zhou Enlai, Zhu De, Deng Xiaoping, Peng Zhen, Chen Yi, Li Fuchun, etc.
3. 12–28 September 1975	Zhu De, Deng Xiaoping, Zhang Chunqiao, Yao Wenyuan, Li Xiannian, etc.	Hua Guofeng, Ye Jianying, Deng Xiaoping, Li Xiannian, etc.
4. 15–30 September 1979	Hua Guofeng, Deng Xiaoping, Li Xiannian, Wang Dongxing, Wang Zhen, etc.	Hua Guofeng, Ye Jianying, Deng Xiaoping, Li Xiannian, etc.

Source: Compiled by the authors.

A Chinese sport expert who used to be a gymnast competed at the First National Games. He described his teammates and his own feelings when they saw Chairman Mao at the opening ceremony of the First National Games in 1959:

> I would never forget the day when I saw Chairman Mao. I was a gymnast and was sent to represent Zhejiang Province to attend the First National Games in 1959. Many young athletes in my team and I could not fall asleep the day before the opening ceremony because we were too eager to see Chairman Mao at the opening ceremony. We were told that if the revolutionary ballad 'The East is Red' was played;[62] Chairman Mao would attend the ceremony. On the opening day, I remember it was three o'clock in the afternoon, 'The East is Red' was played at the BWS. All the audience members stood up to welcome Chairman Mao and other national leaders to the stadium. We were so excited because we saw Chairman Mao sit in the centre of the grandstand. While our delegation parade was facing the grandstand of the stadium, Chairman Mao was waving his hand with a smile on his face. Although it was too far to see clearly, my fighting blood was boiling and some of my teammates were sobbing because we were so excited to meet Chairman Mao in person. . . . We did not know who shouted 'Long Life Chairman Mao; Long Life the PRC', but we echoed, and all the Chinese people in the stadium echoed. . . . At that time, my teammates and I felt so proud

to be Chinese. . . . It was an unforgettable memory in my entire life to meet beloved Chairman Mao.[63]

The response of the audience at the opening ceremony of the National Games showed that the state leaders had got support from people of the Chinese nation. At the same time, the attendance of Chairman Mao, as a uniting figure in the PRC, indicated that ceremonies of the National Games were partly intended as a platform to propagate the state-guiding political ideology.

In addition, for each games, the BWS, as the sports venue, was decorated with political symbols, such as the red flag, the banners and posters and portraits of state leaders. For example, the framed shining portrait of Chairman Mao was hung above the stadium rostrum at BWS. The National Games posters were displayed all around the arena. They made a lasting impression on Chinese athletes and the audience.[64]

For example, the BWS for the Second Games in 1965 was decorated with many large banners with slogans such as 'Hold high the red flag of Mao Zedong thought and advance courageously!', 'The people are of one heart and follow the Chinese Communist Party forever!', and 'Long life Chairman Mao, the red sun in the heart of the revolutionary people in the world!'. The Chinese government utilized poster propaganda at the sport arena for the Third National Games in 1975 to ensure popular support and to further anti-imperialist sentiment among the Chinese nation. For example, posters entitled 'Energetically criticize the Chinese Khrushchev's politics, ideology and theories!'[65] and 'Thoroughly revolutionize battlefronts of ideas and culture!'[66]

Despite that, state leaders were invited to give speeches at opening and closing ceremonies of each games and, sometimes, they voiced support of the National Games by writing poems or inscriptions. For example, Dong Biwu, the Vice-chairman of the PRC, wrote a congratulatory poem for the First Games in 1959, which was entitled 'Ode to the First National Games'; Guo Moruo, the first president of the Chinese Academy of Sciences and the first president of the University of Science and Technology of the PRC, also wrote a poem for the First National Games. The prominent Chinese military leader Marshal Nie Rongzhen also wrote a congratulatory article to felicitate the games.[67]

The delegations' parade and mass calisthenics

Foucault describes the significance of opening ceremonies in sports events as an example of the 'micro-physics of power' that are symptomatic of the modern state.[68] These rituals include the parades of athletes with national flags and national emblems, the act of raising the national flag while the national anthem is played and mass calisthenics (or group calisthenics). The programmes were designed to symbolize the Chinese nation, and members of the Chinese nation were inspired by potent symbols of the nation through these rituals.

The athletic delegations' parade at the opening ceremony of the National Games was followed by the parade of the guard of honour. The members of the guard of honour were from the PLA. The parade of the guard of honour marched into the BWS with music of 'March of the Athletes': eight soldiers lifted up the PRC's national emblem and 240 soldiers held up the national flag. Then athletes' delegations marched into the arena wearing their uniforms and being led by a flag-bearing athlete representing the province or municipality they came from (see Figure 3.4). It was designed by each of the Organizing Committees to display athletes from different delegations to spectators and to show the progress of sport development in China. Moreover, the parade of the Taiwan province delegation at the Third and Fourth National Games symbolically showed the national unity of China. The time of the Third and Fourth National Games were close to China's Mid-autumn Festival, which was seen as a reunion of the Chinese nation in the sports arena.[69]

In China, mass calisthenics has long been taken as a traditional performance at the opening ceremony of sports events at different levels. It is a comprehensive collected square performance, which involves many participants with an integration of sports and artistic forms: movement and modelling, formation design, and art decoration with music, costume, scene and light.[70] Susan Brownell has argued that the body of Chinese people was used by politicians to promote Communist nationalism, and mass calisthenics at the opening ceremonies of the National Games displayed the militarized body training of the young generation for the defence of the Chinese nation in Mao Zedong's era (see Figure 3.5).[71] She concluded that the demonstration of mass calisthenics had always been seen in the Soviet Union and other socialist countries to express collectivism, but not seen in the West since World War II.[72] However, the mass calisthenics was very popular at the ceremonies of the National Games. It was a way to show the CCP's revolutionary history, but more importantly, sports arenas of the National Games, as Faucault states, knit a dense web of power relations, and these sports ceremonies have positive effects on showing it and promoting China's political ideology of national unity under the CCP's leadership.

For instance, mass calisthenics at the ceremony of the Fourth National Games in 1979 was one of the important Communist techniques for inculcating the Chinese state political ideology for a promise of greater stability, prosperity, and a new drive for modernization in the future of China when

Figure 3.4 Parades of the National Games in the PRC, 1959 and 1965
Source: The GASC, 2006, pp. 1 and 27.

China began its economic reform and opening-up policy after 1978. The title was 'A new long march', which symbolized that China would march into a new era that would focus on pragmatic economic reform.

The performance included five acts. The first act, 'Celebrate the victory', was performed by more than 2,000 people with red silk ribbons in their hands,

people watch colourful flowers. The throbbing flowers presented the future (figure 3.5) of Chinese citizens and the nation's bright future guidance of the CCP's path. As athletes marching up. According to their future, as well, the

1965年　第一届全运会在北京举行。图为在开幕式上表演的大型团体操《革命赞歌》第四场《人民公社好》。

Figure 3.5 Mass Calisthenics of the National Games in the PRC, 1959 and 1965
Source: The GASC, 2006, p. 29.

which formed China's national flag (50 metres long and 30 metres wide). The first act was designed to symbolize the Chinese people's enthusiasm to celebrate the 30th anniversary of the PRC. The second act, 'Open up the future', involved 1,200 young girls wearing white blouses and pink skirts under the background of a picture of Monument to the People's Heroes. They waved yellow fans to express the memory of revolutionary martyrs while images of Chairman Mao, Premier Zhou Enlai and Zhu De appeared in the background. The third act, 'Grow healthy and strong', was performed by 1,200 young pioneers with hula hoops who performed different free-standing exercises and children's games. The BWS was decorated by the banner with 'We love science' to show China's young generation's longing to study modern knowledge and high technology in a modern era. The fourth act was called 'Continuously conquer the peak', which was performed by 1,000 gymnasts in the scenes of free gymnastics, techniques and a human pyramid to reflect the Chinese people's determination and willpower to carry forward the fighting spirit. The last act, 'Glorious future', was performed by more than 3,000 people with colourful flowers. The blooming flowers expressed the bright future of Four Modernizations and the nation's faith under guidance of the CCP's policy of reform and opening-up. According to data from the SSM, the number of people involved in group calisthenics (or mass calisthenics) was 15,726, and behind the scenes these performances involved 8,340 people.[73] These performances were designed to symbolize that the Chinese people were filled with hope for the new goals of the Four Modernizations.

Some mass calisthenics teams in other socialist countries in the world, including Chile, Syria and Sudan, had visited and studied in China in the 1970s. In addition, Algeria, Morocco, Togo, Albania, Nigeria, Niger, Madagascar and other countries had invited Chinese sports experts to their countries to train choreographers. The President of Niger personally awarded the Honorary Certificate of Meritorious Service and Knight Medal to some Chinese sports experts to thank them for their help.[74] Hence, the communication of the mass calisthenics also made its contribution in improving China's diplomacy with other countries in the 1970s.

Mass media and the promotion of the National Games

The major media outlets in China were state-run, and they were supervised and censored by the PRC Ministry of Culture under the Chinese central government. The major news agencies involved in reporting the first four National Games included *Xinhua News Agency*, *People's Daily* and the *Central People's Broadcasting Station*, as well as some local news agencies.[75]

People's Daily, for example, printed 165 articles about the First National Games within the 30 days before, during and after the games.[76] The content

of these reports included the ceremonies, competitions, athletes, delegations and so forth. On the opening day of the First National Games, *People's
Daily* published a newspaper editorial entitled 'Create the best performance
to present the best gift for the National Day – Congratulations to the opening ceremony of the First National Games'.[77] This comment illustrated how
the First National Games would display the development of competitive
sport in China and the image of new China: self-reliant, self-confident, with
a love for sport and for life. It also emphasized the choice of athletes: '
athletes were selected from all walks of life – workers, peasants and soldiers, officials, students and businessmen from both Han and different ethnic minorities'.[78] This editorial was a reminder of the spirit of socialism and
national unity in China to the general public.

The media's discourse also communicated the Chinese central government's expectations for the National Games. The mottos of the National
Games were cited by the mass media many times, such as 'Exercise the
body, build our motherland and defend the nation'. The key words of media
reports on the National Games were positive and encouraging, and it is
hard to find any negativity. Reports were peppered with positive words such
as 'wonderful', 'record-breaking', 'big-union', 'distinguished', 'vigour',
'enthusiasm', 'spectacular', 'news of victory', 'harvest', 'renew', 'a milestone', 'high aspirations'.[79] Besides, the CPBS also played an important
role in disseminating the National Games in factories, workshops and even
in rural areas.

Some local news agencies, which were run by local government yet
supervised by the PRC State Ministry of Culture, were also involved in
publicity of the National Games. Since the First National Games was held
to celebrate the 10th anniversary of the PRC in Beijing, *Beijing Daily* and
Beijing Evening News began to report the Games a few months before
they started. It has been estimated that about 400 articles about the games
appeared in the period of the First National Games.[80] Most of the reports
indicate the significance and achievement of the National Games, such as
the competition of different sports events, spirit of the athletes and hard
work of those involved in the games, for instance, referees, service staff
and drivers.[81]

Some descriptions of athletes who broke world records were also very
instructive and encouraging. This is illustrated by a news report on swim-
mer Mu Xiangxiong, one of the superstars at the First National Games in
1959. He broke the world record twice with a result of 1 minute and 11.3
seconds and 1 minute and 11.1 seconds in the men's 100m breaststroke.
Mu was depicted as a national warrior in most media articles and radio
broadcasting. *Beijing Daily* specifically described that Mu Xiangxiong took
a self-critical attitude towards his training in order to "perform better for

our motherland, although he had already created a new world record . . . he was one of the real proletariat soldiers".[82] The comment also stated that he had followed the correct leadership of the CCP and central government and built an indomitable will and a humble personality.[83] In addition, some news reports directly linked politics with the National Games when describing the achievements of the games. This can be exemplified by two reports in *Beijing Daily* entitled, 'The National Games: great achievement in both politics and sport' and 'The National Games: the mighty pyramid of sport under the leadership of the central government'.[84] Both articles highlighted how athletes were trained and improved by the Marxist ideology and political education under the CCP's leadership, as well as how the National Games became a success both in sporting and political terms in China.[85]

In 1965, a special session was held in *Xinhua News Agency* before the Second National Games. The director of *Xinhua* raised four essential points to clarify the regulations and directions of report of the Second National Games in 1965: politics, ideology, collectivism and the masses.[86] For example, he illuminated how to highlight politics through four aspects, including the following:

1   Publicize sport policies made by the CCP and Chairman Mao, clarify the purpose, function and significance of sport in China, as well as combine sport with productivity and national defence;
2   Utilize sport to showcase the priority of the socialist system in China, and link sport achievement with Chinese socialist revolution and socialist construction;
3   Not only cover news about achievement of the games, but also answer why and how the success could happen;
4   Link athletes' performances with the spirit of revolutionary heroism and communism, and eventually to highlight Mao Zedong Thoughts.[87]

With these guidelines, the report from *Xinhua News Agency* not only focused on the spirit of the Games and sports achievements but also publicized Mao Zedong Thought and superiority of the socialist system to the public. For instance, two pieces of news entitled 'Learn from Mao's works and the PLA: athletes in China have a new face' and 'Athletes who attended the National Games have studied and adhered to Mao Zedong Thought'.[88] These two pieces of news illustrated athletes who insisted on learning Mao Zedong Thought, which was the source and power for the development of sport in China. Furthermore, mass media increased reports on military sport at the Second National Games – shooting, skydiving, motorcycling, radio sport, skydiving, aero modeling and marine modeling – to illustrate the significance of military sport to national defence at the time.[89]

People's Daily's report on the Taiwan province delegation at the Third and Fourth National Games also showcased the political stance of the Chinese government and CCP's leadership. During the Third National Games, an article was published entitled 'Welcome blood brothers from Taiwan: interview with athletes from Taiwan province delegation at the Third National Games'.[90] The article had three subtitles: 'Long for Beijing and love the motherland', 'Joyful gathering', and 'A common aspiration of unity'. It can be seen that this article voiced the state political ideology: Taiwan is part of the territory of the PRC. The last sentence of this article, 'we must liberate Taiwan', strongly voiced the position of the Chinese government on the Taiwan issue.[91] There were 11 other articles on the Taiwan province delegation that expressed the insistent political ideology of the Chinese state.[92] In these articles, the use of 'Taiwan province' was a repartee to clearly claim that Taiwan is part of the PRC.

In addition, the sports arena of the National Games became the best site for the making of sports documentaries in China. China Central Newsreel and Documentary Film Studio made a sport documentary *Long Live Youth* in 1959 to celebrate China's 10 years' achievement in sport after the founding of the PRC.[93] In short, state-run media's report on the National Games formed a unique symbiotic relationship between the Chinese government and its people via production and diffusion of national discourse for the Chinese national community.

The National Games and Chinese nationalism

It is known that China's National Games in the late Qing and Republican era (1910–1948) was the forerunner for the games in the PRC era.[94] Hence, the National Games in both eras share some similarities. Firstly, the games in both eras were held at irregular intervals under an unstable social environment in China. Some of the National Games in both eras were linked with the celebration of the National Day to raise patriotic sentiment. For example, in the Republican era, the Fifth and Sixth National Games in 1933 and 1935 were both opened on 10 October when the National Day of the Republic of China was celebrated. In the PRC, the First National Games in 1959 aimed to celebrate the 10th anniversary of the PRC, and it was regarded as a tribute project to display great achievements in socialist China leading by the CCP. Secondly, some of the National Games in both eras were utilized by the Chinese government to create a sense of unified national identity. They were also linked with militarism and the rejection of the perceived humiliation in the anti-imperialist context. Thirdly, the National Games in both eras attracted many journalists and photographers from different newspapers and news agencies. This is particularly true of the state-run news agencies in the PRC era, where the representations of the patriotic and anti-imperialist sentiment at the National Games were reported and spread throughout the public within China.

However, several notable differences merit further discussion. In the Republican era, the establishment of the 1910 and 1914 National Games by the YMCA was intended to imitate the Olympic Games to achieve sports modernity, which more or less reflected the Western cultural imperialism project in modern China. With the effort of the Chinese nationalists, China regained the sports sovereignty from the Westerners via hosting the 1924 National Games, which was a turning point in the process of indigenizing Western sports ideology in China. With the support of the Nationalist government, another four National Games in the 1930s and 1940s were organized by the China National Amateur Athletic Federation (CNAAF), a non-governmental sports organization, and utilized to promote anti-imperialist and patriotic sentiment. Despite these gains, the National Games did not establish a systematic governance or managerial structure in the context of constant foreign invasions, frequent civil wars as well as unstable political and economic climate. Thus, the late Qing and Republican era (1910–1948) could only be identified as the infancy years of the National Games in China.

After the founding of the PRC, however, the Chinese government formulated a well-structured sports system for the development of both mass and elite sport to fulfil its political and diplomatic demands.[95] The National Games in 1959 were restored by the Chinese government as a national programme of celebration. The first four National Games were supervised and funded by the Chinese government, and it was a state-led sports event in China. The SSM was the national sports governing body under the State Council, which directly organized these four National Games. At the same time, the Chinese government gradually formed and developed a well-organized managerial system of the National Games and established a favourable foundation for future games in China.

Chinese nationalism was a continuous driving force behind the development of the first four National Games in the PRC. These games also reflected the changing focus of Chinese nationalism, especially the state-led nationalism in China. In the early 1950s, Chinese nationalistic sentiment and national identity in sport were triggered by the 'two Chinas' issue at the Helsinki Olympic Games in 1952. The PRC withdrew from the IOC and other international sports federations in 1958 to protect its sole legitimacy. Meanwhile, the Chinese government was conscious of the diplomatic function of sport in achieving the international recognition of the new regime and its legitimacy.[96] Influenced by the Great Leap Forward, the First National Games was not only designed to demonstrate China's 10 years' achievement through communist ideology and China's self-reliance policy, but also mobilized the general public to participate in the games for the purpose of national construction and national defence. In the 1960s, China faced the Sino-India conflict, the Sino-Soviet split and the Vietnam War, which resulted in a rise in the significance of sports militarism for national sovereignty. On the one hand, the Second National Games prepared Chinese athletes to attend the GANEFO to challenge Western hegemony in sport; while on the other hand, the Games were utilized to publicize the importance of class struggle, socialist revolution and mass military training in preparation for war. Through the nationwide preliminaries and mass calisthenics for the National Games, many military sports events and militarized training philosophy were popularized in Chinese society.

The Cultural Revolution gave rise to both nativist anti-Western xenophobia and anti-traditionalist sentiment in China;[97] however, in sport Ping-Pong Diplomacy in the early 1970s was a turning point for the Chinese government to be converged with the Western world. The Third National Games also aimed to prepare Chinese elite athletes to participate in future international sports events to display China's new image to the rest of the world. At the same time, the Chinese government tactically gave support to establish a Taiwan province delegation to stand for national sovereignty and territorial integrity at the Third and the Fourth National Games. They displayed a close relationship between elite sport and Chinese politics and diplomacy. Moreover, the Fourth National Games was held at the eve of China's changing political ideology from Mao Zedong's class struggle to pursuing economic modernization through Deng Xiaoping's reform and opening-up policy, a more pragmatic way. In line with this pragmatic nationalism, a national interest-driven approach, which would focus on economic construction and the Four Modernizations, the Fourth National Games also changed its slogans to highlight modernization in China.

The promotion of the Games also displayed the politicization of the first four National Games. Benedict Anderson articulated that the printed media, the newspaper, facilitated the construction of nationalism and national consciousness.[98] The same newspaper has created common understandings and shared interests, which have unified members of a national community even if they have never met or will never meet.[99] The National Games were also deliberately disseminated via the same state-run media to the Chinese populace, which facilitated defending the party's right and overthrowing the hostile attitudes and arguments of its opponents.[100] The leading articles and comments of the National Games also reflected that the National Games was not merely a sports event but also a useful lens through which the changing focus of Chinese nationalism could be identified. The state-run media made full use of the National Games to disseminate the Chinese government's voice in the right direction. Consequently, a social cohesion and unity was built.

By socio-historical investigation of the governance, operation and promotion of the National Games in the early PRC, it is notable that nationalism was still a driving force behind the development of this mega-sports event in the early stage of the PRC. In contrast to the National Games in the Republican era, the involvement of the Chinese government as well as a relatively stable social circumstance from 1949 to 1979, however, helped the National Games form a well-structured management mechanism and established a fundamental governing and operational system for the future games in China. Meanwhile, by virtue of China's state-run media, the hosting of the National Games in this period has existed as a medium through which various political appeals and demands have been made by the Chinese government, such as to strengthen national defence, solidarity and cohesion, as well as to reinforce its political legitimacy. It is arguable that the promotion of the National Games in the early PRC was a vehicle par excellence for showing national unity and solidarity to people within and outside of China.

Notes

1 Zedong Mao, *Selected Works of Mao Zedong*, Volume. 5 (Beijing: Foreign Languages Press, 1977), 17.
2 Gries, 'China and Chinese Nationalism', 488–499.
3 Wenfang Tang, and Benjamin Darr, 'Chinese Nationalism and its Political and Social Origins', *Journal of Contemporary China* 21, no. 77 (2012): 813; Zhao, *A Nation-State by Construction*.
4 Zhao, 'Chinese Nationalism and its International Orientations', 1–33.
5 Zhao, *A Nation-State by Construction*, 251.
6 Zedong Mao, *Selected Works of Mao Zedong*, Volume. 2 (Beijing: Foreign Language Press, 1965), 381.
7 The Four Olds included Old Customs, Old Culture, Old Habits and Old Ideas. It became one of the goals of the Cultural Revolution to bring an end to the Four Olds.
8 Brownell, *Training the Body for China*, 34–66.
9 Wenbin Feng, 'New Democratic National Sport in the PRC', New Sports, July 1, 1950: 8–9.
10 Barrie Houlihan and Mick Green, eds., *Comparative Elite Sport Development* (Burlington: Routledge, 2007), 36.
11 After 1979 when the PRC had resumed its seat in the IOC, the COC was separated from the ACSF to legally represent the PRC in the IOC.
12 Hong Fan and Zhouxiang Lu, 'China', in Matthew Nicholism, Russell Hoye and Barrie Houlihan, eds., *Participation in Sport International Policy Perspective* (New York: Routledge, 2010): 162–182.
13 The Great Leap Forward was launched in order to implement Mao's slogan 'greater, faster, better, more economical', which was put forward from 1958 to 1960. This campaign aimed to rapidly change the nation from an agrarian

economy to a socialist, collectivized and industrialized society. However, the Great Leap Forward resulted in an economic regression and also destroyed the Chinese statistical system.

14 Archive of General Administration of Sport in China (GASC), *The Ten-Year Guidelines for Sports Development 1958–1967* (Beijing: The Sports Ministry, 9 February 1958).

15 Archive of GASC, *Report on the Ten-Year Guidelines for Sports Development* (Beijing: The Sports Ministry, September 8, 1958).

16 It is one of the main principles of training of competitive sports of the PRC, and it means 'training rigorously, intensively, competitively and with high volume training'.

17 The full name of the Cultural Revolution is the Great Proletarian Cultural Revolution from 1966 to 1976. It was a social political movement in Mao's era. The aim of this movement was to preserve the communist ideology and to destroy the remnants of capitalist and traditional elements from Chinese society. Hsu, *Rise of Modern China*, 324–327.

18 Hong Fan, 'Two Roads to China: The Inadequate and Adequate', *The International Journal of History of Sports* 18, no. 2 (2001): 148–167.

19 Ibid., 158–159.

20 Zhuang Zedong (25 August 1940–10 February 2013) was a Chinese table tennis player, and he was three-time winner of the world men's singles and champion of numerous other table tennis events.

21 Fan and Lu, 'Representing the New China and the Sovietisation of Chinese Sport (1949–1962)', 8.

22 Yannon Fu, ed., *China's Sport History* (1949–1979) (Beijing: Beijing: People's Sport Press, 2008), 36.

23 The State Sport Ministry, *Collection of Sports Policy Documents (1949–1981)* (Beijing: Beijing: People's Sport Press, 1982), 30.

24 Ibid., 34.

25 David B. Kanin, *Political History of the Olympic Games* (Boulder, CO: Westview Press, 1981), 112–119.

26 Rusli Lutan and Hong Fan, 'The Politicization of Sport: GANEFO – a Case Study', *Sport in Society* 8, no. 3 (2005): 425–439.

27 Ibid.

28 Ibid.

29 'The Opening Ceremony of the Second National Games', *People's Daily*, September 11, 1965, 5.

30 The State Sport Ministry, 'The Sport Ministry's Proposal of Hosting the Second National Games', in *Collection of Sports Policy Documents* (Beijing: Beijing People's Press, 1982): 883.

31 'The Classic Poster of the Second National Games', *Sohu Sport*, August 25, 2013, accessed March 21, 2015, http://pic.sports.sohu.com/group-473021.shtml#0.

32 Suisheng Zhao, 'Chinese Nationalism and Its International Orientations', *Political Science Quarterly* 115, no. 1 (2000): 1–33.

33 The GASC, *The 10 National Games of China* (Beijing: People's Sports Publishing House of China, 2006), 21.

34 'Four Modernizations' was announced by Deng Xiaoping at the Third Plenum of the 11th Central Committee. It included the modernization of agriculture, industry, technology and defense.

35 Fu, ed., *Chinese Sport History 1949–1979*, 407–409.
36 Brian Graham, 'Heritage as Knowledge: Capital or Culture?', *Urban Studies* 39, nos. 5–6 (2002): 1003–1017.
37 Shaozu Wu et al., *Sport History in the PRC 1949–1998* (Beijing: China Ancient Books Publishing House, 1999), 204.
38 Hong Fan and Zhouxiang Lu, 'Sport, Militarism and Diplomacy: Training Bodies for China (1960–1966)', *The International Journal of the History of Sport* 29, no. 1 (2012): 30–52.
39 Henry Kissinger, 'The Stakes with China', *The Washington Post*, March 31, 1996, 7.
40 Shulong Chu, 'National Unity, Sovereignty and Territorial Integration', *The China Journal* (1996): 98–102.
41 Kurt M. Campbell and Mitchell J. Derek, 'Crisis in the Taiwan Strait', *Foreign Affairs* 80, no. 4 (2001): 14–25; Thomas J. Christensen, 'The Contemporary Security Dilemma: Deterring a Taiwan Conflict', *Washington Quarterly* 25, no. 4 (2002): 5–21.
42 Alan M. Wachman, *Why Taiwan? Geostrategic Rationales for China's Territorial Integrity* (Singapore: National University of Singapore, 2008), 25–44.
43 Junwei Yu, 'China's Foreign Policy in Sport: The Primacy of National Security and Territorial Integrity Concerning the Taiwan Question', *The China Quarterly* no. 194 (2008): 294–308.
44 From the Chinese government (lead by the CCP)'s point of view, Taiwan is a local province of the PRC.
45 Fu, ed., *Sport History in China 1949–1979*, 298–302.
46 'The Taiwan Delegation for the Third National Games was Established in Beijing Today', *Xinhua News Agency*, August 23, 1975, accessed January 15, 2015, www.71.cn/2012/0410/560744.shtml.
47 'Enjoy the Same Moon and Drink Water from the Same River', *Chengshi Kuaibao*, October 27, 2005, accessed January 15, 2015, http://sports.sina.com.cn/o/2005-10-27/18081847723.shtml.
48 'Enjoy the Same Moon and Drink from the Same River', *Xinhua Daily*, September 20, 1975, 7.
49 The poem in Chinese is '天府黄柚如蜜甜，溯源台省百年前。吃柚甜甜念宝岛，球场言欢话团圆。峨眉玉山相对颜，嘉陵浊溪一水连。手足同心齐努力，赢来宝岛换人间。' This poem expressed the poet's good wish for the reunification of China. 'Enjoy the Same Moon and Drink from the Same River', *Xinhua Daily*, 7.
50 Michael Oksenburg, 'China's Confident Nationalism', *Foreign Affairs* 65, no. 3 (1986): 501–523.
51 From interview material in China.
52 Fu, ed., *Sport History in China 1949–1979*, 135.
53 Brownell, *Training the Body for China*, 135–136.
54 Smith, *Nations and Nationalism in a Global Era*, 28.
55 Zedong Mao, 'Talks at the Yenan Forum on Art and Literature', in *Selected Works of Mao Zedong* (Beijing: People's Publishing House, 1978): 250.
56 'Li' is a unit of Chinese measurement and one Li equals 500 metres.
57 Zhongyu Wen, 'The Fourth National Games in the PRC', *Journal of Sport Culture Guide* no. 2 (1983): 17.
58 Ibid., 18.

59 For health reasons, they were not present at the ceremonies of the Third National Games in 1975 during their lifetime, but Martial Zhu De attended to represent the Chinese state government.
60 'Review the Achievements in Sport in the Past 10 Years; the First National Games was launched', *People's Daily*, September 14, 1959, 1.
61 Zhang Jianhui, *Chinese National Games' Institutional Change: Order, Identity and Profit* (Beijing: Beijing Sport University Press, 2011), 103.
62 'The East is Red' was a song with lyrics that idealize Mao Zedong, and Mao's popularization of the song was one of his earliest efforts to promote his image as a perfect hero in Chinese popular culture, especially during the Cultural Revolution period. The English translation of the song is: 'The east is red, the sun rises. From China arises Mao Zedong. He strives for people's happiness, Hurrah; he is the people's great saviour. Chairman Mao loves the people. He is our guide to building a new China, Hurrah, lead us forward. The Communist Party is like the sun. Wherever it shines, it is bright. Wherever the Communist Party is, hurrah, there the people are liberated.'
63 From interview material in China.
64 Julia F. Andrews, *Painters and Politics in the People's Republic of China, 1949–1979* (Auckland: University of California Press, 1994), 256–340.
65 Mao Zedong dubbed Liu Shaoqi 'the Chinese Khrushchev' to identify him as a national enemy. Liu Shaoqi was considered the CCP's chief political rival and so he was imprisoned in 1968 and died in 1969. Roderick MacFarquhar, *The Origins of the Cultural Revolution*, Volume 3 (New York: Oxford University Press, 1997).
66 Julia F. Andrews, 'The Art of the Cultural Revolution', in Richard King, ed., *Art in Turmoil: The Chinese Cultural Revolution, 1966–76* (Seattle: University of Washington Press, 2010): 27–57.
67 Xiaozheng Xiong and Zhong Binshu, eds., *Sport in the PRC 1949–2009* (Beijing: Beijing: Sports University, 2010), 56–57.
68 Michel Foucault, *Discipline and Punish* (New York: Vintage, 1979), 135–141.
69 The Mid-autumn Festival, which takes place on 15 August in the Chinese lunar calendar, is the traditional festival to celebrate the gathering or reunion of family and friends.
70 Kuanrou Huang, Xuexin Mao and Xin Wu, 'The Historical Development of Chinese Group Calisthenics', *The International Journal of the History of Sport* 28, no. 7 (2011): 1072–1085.
71 Brownell, *Training the Body for China*, 136–143.
72 Ibid., 315.
73 Wen, 'The Fourth National Games in the PRC', 19.
74 Huang, Mao and Wu, 'The Historical Development of Chinese Group Calisthenics', 1072–1085.
75 *The Xinhua News Agency* is the state press agency of the PRC and is a ministry-level department subordinate to the State Council. It is the sole channel for the distribution of important news relating to the CCP and Chinese central government. *People's Daily*, an official newspaper of the central government of China, was one of the most powerful and influential nationwide newspapers. *China National Radio*, also known as *Central People's Broadcasting Station*, is the national radio station of the PRC, and its headquarters are in Beijing. It was the main broadcasting news channel for the entire national audience.

76 Chinese Academy of Social Science, *Yearbook of Chinese Journalism 1990* (Beijing: China Social Sciences Publishing House, 1990).
77 'Create the Best Performance to Present the Best Gift for the National Day', *People's Daily*, September 13, 1959, 5.
78 Ibid.
79 Editorial Team of the Chinese Academy of Social Science, ed., *Yearbook of Chinese Journalism 1990* (Beijing: China Social Sciences Publishing House, 1990).
80 Shi Jun, 'Review of the Report of the National Games from Beijing Daily and Beijing Evening News', *Xinwen Zhanxian (新闻战线)* no. 20 (1959): 25.
81 Ibid., 26.
82 Caizhen Zhang, ed., *Yearbook of Chinese Sport 1949–1991* (Beijing: People's Sport Press, 1993), 476–502; Beijing Evening News, 'Mu Xiangxiong Created World Records at the First National Games', *Beijing Evening News*, September 18, 1959, 3.
83 Beijing Evening News, 'Mu Xiangxiong Created World Records at the First National Games', 3.
84 'The National Games: Great Achievement in Both Politics and Sport', *Beijing Daily*, October 2, 1959, 2; 'The National Games: The Mighty Pyramid of Sport under the Leadership of the Central Government', *Beijing Daily*, October 4, 1959, 1.
85 Shi Jun, 'Review of the Report of the National Games from Beijing Daily and Beijing Evening News', *Xinwen Zhanxian (新闻战线)* no. 20 (1959): 27.
86 Wen Hua, 'Sport News Must Highlight Politics: The Overview of the Report of the Second National Games', *Xinwen Yewu (新闻业务)* no. 21 (1965): 32.
87 Ibid.
88 Ibid.
89 Ibid.
90 'Welcome Blood Brothers from Taiwan: Interview Athletes from Taiwan Delegation at the Third National Games', *People's Daily*, September 11, 1975, 3.
91 Ibid.
92 Yao Zhang, 'Research on the National Games Report by People's Daily' (MA thesis, Beijing Sport University, Beijing, China, 2011), 34–35.
93 Fu, ed., *The Sport History in China 1949–1979*, 269–270.
94 Liu Li and Fan Hong, 'The National Games and National Identity in the Republic of China 1910–1948', *International Journal of the History of Sport* 3, no. 32 (2015): 440–454.
95 Lu and Fan, *Sport and Nationalism in China*, 99.
96 Ibid., 78–83.
97 Zhao, 'Chinese Nationalism and Its International Orientations', 1–33.
98 Anderson, *Imagined Communities*, 44.
99 Ibid., 19.
100 Karl Marx and Friedrich Engels, *Collected Works: Vol. 10, Marx and Engels: 1849–1851* (London: Lawrence & Wishart, 1975).

References

Anderson, Benedict. *Imagined Communities: Reflections on the Origin and Spread of Nationalism*. London: Verso Books, 2006.
Andrews, Julia F. *Painters and Politics in the People's Republic of China, 1949–1979*. Auckland: University of California Press, 1994.

Brownell, Susan. *Training the Body for China: Sports in the Moral Order of the People's Republic*. Chicago: University of Chicago Press, 1995.

Fan, Hong, and Zhouxiang Lu. 'Representing the New China and the Sovietisation of Chinese Sport (1949–1962).' *The International Journal of the History of Sport* 29, no. 1 (2012): 1–29.

Fan, Hong, and Zhouxiang Lu. 'Sport, Militarism and Diplomacy: Training Bodies for China (1960–1966).' *The International Journal of the History of Sport* 29, no. 1 (2012): 30–52.

Fan, Hong. 'Two Roads to China: The Inadequate and the Adequate (Review Essay).' *The International Journal of the History of Sport* 18, no. 2 (2001): 148–167.

Fu, Yannon, ed. *China's Sport History 1949–1979*. Beijing: People's Sport Press, 2008.

The GASC. *The 10 National Games of China*. Beijing: People's Sports Publishing House of China, 2006.

Graham, Brian. 'Heritage as Knowledge: Capital or Culture?' *Urban Studies* 39, nos. 5–6 (2002): 1003–1017.

Gries, Peter Hays. 'China and Chinese Nationalism.' In *The Sage Handbook of Nations and Nationalism*, edited by Gerard Delanty and Krishan Kumar, 488–499. London and Thousand Oaks: Sage, 2006.

Houlihan, Barrie, and Mick Green, eds. *Comparative Elite Sport Development*. Burlington: Routledge, 2007.

Hsu, Immanuel C. Y. *Rise of Modern China*. Oxford: Oxford University Press, 1975.

Huang, Kuanrou, Xuexin Mao, and Xin Wu. 'The Historical Development of Chinese Group Calisthenics.' *The International Journal of the History of Sport* 28, no. 7 (2011): 1072–1085.

Jianhui, Zhang. *Chinese National Games' Institutional Change: Order, Identity and Profit*. Beijing: Beijing Sport University Press, 2011.

Kanin, David B. *Political History of the Olympic Games*. Boulder, CO: Westview Press, 1981.

King, Richard, ed. *Art in Turmoil: The Chinese Cultural Revolution, 1966–76*. Seattle: University of Washington Press, 2010.

Lutan, Rusli, and Hong Fan. 'The Politicization of Sport: GANEFO–a Case Study.' *Sport in Society* 8, no. 3 (2005): 425–439.

Mao, Zedong. *Selected Works of Mao Zedong*, Vol. 5. Beijing: Foreign Languages Press, 1977.

Nicholism, Matthew, Russell Hoye, and Barrie Houlihan, eds. *Participation in Sport International Policy Perspective*. New York: Routledge, 2010.

Oksenburg, Michael. 'China's Confident Nationalism.' *Foreign Affairs* 65, no. 3 (1986): 501–523.

Smith, Anthony D. *Nations and Nationalism in a Global Era*. Malden, MA: Polity Press, 2013.

The State Sport Ministry. *Collection of Sports Policy Documents (1949–1981)*. Beijing: People's Sport Press, 1982.

Wachman, Alan M. *Why Taiwan? Geostrategic Rationales for China's Territorial Integrity*. Singapore: National University of Singapore, 2008.

Wu, Shaozu, et al. *Sports History of the People's Republic of China 1949–1999*. Beijing: China Archives Publishing House, 1999.

Xiong, Xiaozheng, and Bingshu Zhong, eds. *The 60 Years' History of Sport in China 1949–2009*. Beijing: Beijing Sport University Press, 2010.

Yu, Junwei. 'China's Foreign Policy in Sport: The Primacy of National Security and Territorial Integrity Concerning the Taiwan Question.' *The China Quarterly* 194, no. 194 (2008): 294–308.

Zhang, Caizhen, ed. *Yearbook of Chinese Sport 1949–1991*. Beijing: People's Sport Press, 1993.

Zhao, Suisheng. *A Nation-State by Construction: Dynamics of Modern Chinese Nationalism*. Stanford: Stanford University Press, 2004.

Zhao, Suisheng. 'Chinese Nationalism and Its International Orientations.' *Political Science Quarterly* 115, no. 1 (2000): 1–33.

4 The National Games and China's Olympic Strategy in the post-1980s

Introduction

When the world entered a new era of globalization in the 1980s, there arose increasing global trends towards economic restructuring, technological shifts and cultural regeneration. As Anthony Giddens claimed, 'the emergence of globalized orders . . . means that the world we live "in" today is different from that of previous ages'.[1] The notion of globalization was regarded as 'one single world or human society, in which all regional, national, and local elements are tied together in one interdependent whole'.[2] The worldwide economic, political, cultural and technological globalization affected the emerging economy of China. China's priority was to build the socialist market economy and to achieve the four socialist modernizations of agriculture, industry, science and technology, along with military modernization, by 2000.[3] This socialist transformation for achieving these objectives was called Socialism with Chinese Characteristics.[4] It signified a new era in Chinese history, which focused on economic construction.[5] It has been argued that the post-1980s era in China had been unfolding in line with globalization, marketization, decentralization, privatization, political institutionalization, as well as with financial and legal changes.[6]

The change of the economic system transformed the national sports system accordingly. The PRC's return to the IOC in 1979 and to other international sport federations also marked the beginning of sports globalization in China.[7] The characteristics of sports globalization were considered to be virtually the same as the 'change of sports system, the involvement of the media, dependence on sponsorship, the growth of a sport industry and engagement with transnational corporation'.[8] In China after the 1980s, the sports organizations that were developed under previous centrally planned regimes were now expected to be more economically self-sufficient.

China's success in mega-sports events was regarded as a form of soft power for the nation-state and the rising of 'international prestige, status, and legitimacy'.[9] As Xu Guoqi notes:

> China's participation and even interest in modern sport has been largely motivated by nationalism. But by importing modern sports from the West and taking part in world competitions, China has simultaneously used sports to express its worldview, promote its status in the world, and declare its national identity.[10]

The sports arena became the best generator to exhibit China's economic and political progress. The participation in international sports events was also a representation of the Chinese government's wise political choice of integration into the world community. It was not long before the Chinese government increased its budget for elite sport and formulated the Olympic Strategy to maintain success in the Olympic Games. The Olympic Strategy, which was put forward in 1985, was a turning point in Chinese sports history. The strategy was determined to eradicate the stereotype of the Chinese 'sick man of East Asia' and the humiliation of China as a weak nation, as well as to achieve greater prestige in sport.[11] In order to serve the Olympic Strategy, China established some new sports policies, including implementation of the 'Elite Sport is the Priority' system, JuguoTizhi (also known as 'whole country support elite sport system'), as well as the Olympic Glory Plan.

Chinese nationalism had been enthusiastically expressed at international sports competitions, Olympics, World Championships, World Cups and other international sport scenes after China's opening-up.[12] They were occasions where Chinese people could witness the glory of China, feel proud to be Chinese and feel part of the sense of unity of a great nation.[13]

Driven by its great public exposure, the stakes of involvement in the Olympic Games was higher than other sports events for the production of national culture for international consumption.[14] Moreover, in China, as Susan Brownell observed, the Olympic Games 'gave the overall impression of an attempt to symbolically link economic modernization, Chinese nationalism and Communist Party legitimacy into a meaningful and even moving totality'.[15]

Meanwhile, China also formulated its mass sports policy to balance the development and distribution of the national sports budget between elite sport and mass sport. On 20 June 1995, *An Outline of the National Fitness Program 1995–2010* was approved by the State Council to promote mass sport at a grassroots level in China.[16] This outline turned out to be a milestone in the history of mass sport in China. It had been drawn up with a view to comprehensively promoting mass sport, improving the people's physiques and spurring the socialist modernization of the Chinese nation in the next 15 years.[17]

The Olympic Strategy clarified the relationship between the hosting of the National Games and the attending of the Olympic Games: 'train athletes at home' (the National Games) and 'compete against the foreign competitions' (the Olympic Games). Thus, in line with the implementation of the Olympic Strategy and the globalization of sport in China in the post-1980s, the National Games had its remarkable transformation in many aspects.

New target of the National Games

Guttmann stated that 'international sports events are . . . opportunity for newly independent states to make known their presence to a world that customarily pays them little attention (except to report their natural or man-made disasters)'.[18] The Chinese government took the opportunities of hosting the National Games to prepare Chinese athletes for the Olympics so they could achieve a high ranking at the medal tally.[19] In the 1980s, both the Fifth and Sixth National Games were held a year before the Olympic Games, which focused on serving the forthcoming Olympic Games. This was illustrated by its motto, 'Go beyond Asia and join the advanced world ranks', which expressed the Chinese government's desire to utilize the National Games for political purposes.

However, after suffering setbacks at the Seoul Olympics in 1988, the Chinese sports authorities began to work out a series of approaches based on the requirements of the Olympic Games so as to achieve better performance in the future.[20] In cooperation with the Olympic Strategy, the Chinese government determined to hold the National Games a year after the Summer Olympic Games rather than a year before to guarantee Chinese athletes' best performance at the Olympics. Because the Barcelona Olympic Games was scheduled to be held in 1992, the Seventh National Games was postponed until 15–24 August 1993.

In the 1990s, the competitive sports at the National Games were designed the same as the Olympic sports and were adjusted in line with the forthcoming Olympic Games.[21] Moreover, the National Games changed its staging cities for China's first bidding of the Olympic Games in 1993. Originally, it was decided that the Seventh National Games would be held in Chengdu, the capital city of the Sichuan province, but this was changed to a co-staging operation in Beijing, Sichuan and Qinhuangdao. This was due to the pragmatic Chinese government's political tactics: the wish to display Beijing's ability to stage the Olympic Games to the world via the hosting of the National Games.

On 13 July 2001, the Chinese government won the bid for hosting the 2008 Olympic Games. This was regarded as a landmark in Chinese sports history as well as a major achievement for the Chinese nation.[22] Following Beijing's success, the Ninth National Games was held in Guangzhou in November 2001. This Games was regarded as a 'testing ground' for Chinese national teams for the 2004 Athens Olympic Games. It was hoped to make the Ninth National Games a 'civilized, wonderful, satisfactory sports gala, to make this Games a high prelude for the successful hosting of the 2008 Beijing Olympic Games'.[23]

To summarize, 'Implement the Olympic Strategy and win glory for the motherland' and 'Train the athletes at home and compete against the foreign competitors' became the main principles of elite sport in China as well as the guidelines of the National Games since the 1980s. The National Games was incorporated into China's Olympic Strategy. In other words, as the largest domestic sports event in China, the National Games became the best stage to achieve the requirement of 'Train the athletes at home'. It provided Chinese elite athletes with a training and testing ground to prepare for the Olympics or other international sports events so they could go on to win the glory, prestige and confidence for China and to enhance the Chinese national identity. Correspondingly, the managerial structure and operation system of the National Games changed to meet China's Olympic Strategy's demand.

Reformed structure of time and the staging sites

It has been mentioned that the Fifth (1983) and Sixth (1987) National Games were held a year prior to the Olympic Games. It was soon discovered, however, that one year was not long enough to train the best young athletes for the following year's Olympic Games. To some extent, China's loss in the 1988 Olympic Games indicated that the National Games played a role that was less effective than it was expected to be in maintaining the Olympic success. In order to select the best athletes to perform at the Olympic Games, the hosting time of the National Games was rescheduled to three years before the forthcoming Olympic Games. Hence, the Seventh National Games was postponed from 1991 to 1993, three years before the 1996 Atlanta Olympic Games. This provided more time for the selected young talents at the National Games to prepare for the forthcoming Olympics.[24]

Along with the alteration in the National Games' dates, the staging cities were also changed in light of the Olympic bidding process, from cities directly appointed by the Chinese central government to a bidding system. The selection of a host city for the National Games had to be based on what essential facilities the city could provide, the sports arenas, the accommodation, as well as the transportation system. The first four National Games, from 1959 to 1979, were appointed to be held in Beijing, the capital city of China. This was not only because Beijing represented the new communist regime, but also because Beijing was the only city with the financial capacity and existing facilities to stage the National Games.

In the 1980s and 1990s, Shanghai and Guangzhou became two windows to showcase the economic achievement that China had after the reform and opening-up. These two cities were the new image spokesmen of China's socialist economic modernization. Shanghai and Guangzhou were tactically nominated as the hosting cities of the National Games in 1983 and 1987; however, there was no policy to clarify the hosting cities of the National Games. Inspired by the Olympic bidding system in selecting staging sites as well as the boosting economic growth in local areas and the further commercialization of sport, more cities under provincial governments in China were equipped with reliable and efficient financial capability, facilities and infrastructure for the staging of the National Games. Finally, in December 2000, the State Council approved the Bidding System of the National Games. This approval marked the beginning of the bidding system of the National Games. It also indicated that future National Games were expected to be financially independent. The state government only provided some financial allocations to the competition programme itself, but not for building or improving sports venues and the infrastructure of the hosting cities.[25]

Moreover, inspired by the Olympic bidding system, the local provincial government also had a bidding system for its subordinate city or regional governments to encourage more cities to be involved in the games. It could make full use of the existing sports facilities and expand the influence of the National Games in more cities of the host province. For example, for the staging of the 10th National Games in Jiangsu province, the Nanjing Olympic Sport Complex was determined as the main venue for most of the sports events, and 13 other cities and nine counties also got the chance to stage some sports events by bidding system.[26] This reduced the pressure on the main hosting provincial capital city; meanwhile, more local cities could also be involved in the games.

Reformed competitive sports

The reformed competitive sports of the National Games illustrated its close association with the Olympic Games. Sport in China entered an era of internationalization and globalization after China rejoined the IOC and other international sports federations. Accordingly, the competitive sports at the National Games were readjusted to meet the requirements of China's Olympic Strategy. The Fifth National Games arranged 25 Olympic sports and one demonstration sport – Chinese Wushu. The Seventh National Games in 1993 covered 34 Olympic sports and 9 non-Olympic sports. In order to give priority to the Olympic Strategy, the SSM held a national sport conference in 1993 and issued a directive to implement the reform of the competitive sports. This meant that only Olympic sports and Chinese Wushu were incorporated into the National Games as competitive sports and that the performance sports events were cancelled. Therefore, besides Chinese Wushu, from the Eighth National Games in 1997, all non-Olympic sports were cancelled. This practice shows that the National Games became a 'training and testing ground' to serve the Olympic Games.

Despite the Olympic sports events, Chinese Wushu was retained as a competitive sports event at the National Games. This was mainly because Wushu was regarded as an essential Chinese culture form representative of Chinese national identity. The International Wushu Federation and Chinese Wushu Association have been trying to lobby for Wushu to be included in the official Olympic competitive sports events since 2001, but it has yet to be approved by the IOC.

Fundraising and the scoring system

To stimulate enthusiasm of the local government's participation in the National Games and to mobilize the local government's investment in sport, the state government made a series of policies on the scoring and awarding of points to athletes and their representative local provinces to balance the contradiction between the *Olympic Strategy* at national level and the *National Games Strategy* at local level. Firstly, in 1991 it was announced that from the 1992 Barcelona Olympic Games, medals of athletes obtained from the Olympic Games were incorporated into the scoring system of the National Games. This policy was carried out from the 1993 National Games. It stimulated the local government to give more support to Olympic sports. Secondly, a *Temporary Athletes Exchange Policy* was issued in 1996 to allow athletes to represent a province or municipality other than their own in which to compete. This meant that delegations (i.e. the delegation an athlete originated from *and* the delegation he/she competed for) could negotiate the scoring they received.[27] This policy – *Athletes Exchange Policy* – was officially implemented from the Eighth National Games in 1997. This approach optimized the allocation of athletes for the National Games, which gave more opportunities for elite athletes from different provinces to compete at the National Games. For example, Shanghai had many strong swimmers in their team. Many swimmers' performances in Shanghai were higher than other provinces or municipalities within China. However, the athletes in Hubei Province were better at gymnastics than swimming. Many ranking gymnasts did not have the opportunity to compete at the National Games. This phenomenon could be eliminated if some of Shanghai's ranking swimming athletes exchanged to Hubei Province and vice versa. Both Shanghai and Hubei Province could negotiate the scoring (协议计分) for both delegations at the National Games. Thus, it motivated the positivity of local government's support of the Olympic Strategy to win national glory for China.

Theme songs of the National Games: a longing for the Olympic Games

From the Sixth National Games in 1987, each of the Organizing Committees of the National Games began to produce an official theme song for the games, like the Olympics did. Similar to the Olympic theme songs, these songs were imbued with cultural elements of the Chinese nation or regions (see Table 4.1).

Table 4.1 Theme Songs of the National Games in the PRC[28]

Edition	Title of the Theme Song
The Sixth National Games in 1987	Light of Chinese Nation 中华之光
The Seventh National Games in 1993	China Five Stars invite the Five Olympic Rings 五星邀五环
The Eighth National Games in 1997	A Flying Life 生命的放飞
The Ninth National Games in 2001	Here Comes the Rainbow Again 又见彩虹
The 10th National Games in 2005	Let Time Cheer for Us 让时代为我们喝彩
The 11th National Games in 2009	Love Each Other 相亲相爱

Source: Compiled by the authors.

Moreover, the theme songs of the National Games featured simple and memorable lyrics that people could sing along to. The lyrics of these theme songs reflected the concept of Chinese political ideologies on sport at the time. For instance, the lyrics to the anthem of the Seventh National Games were:

> *Five stars invite the five rings; Beijing connects the world,*
> *China is opening, the Great Wall is embracing.*
> *The sacred torch is burning high to crown thousands of miles with splendour,*
> *The glorious flag is flying high and filled with love from sons and daughters of the Chinese nation.*
> *Five stars invite the five rings; Yangtze River connects the world,*
> *China is opening; Mount Emei is embracing.*

> *Doves of peace are flying high to welcome the revitalization of the new era,*
> *Flowers of friendship are flourishing to applaud the medal-winning athletes.*
> *To tell the blue sky, to tell the earth, we are marching to the future,*
> *To tell the world, to tell the time, we are running to the future,*
> *We are marching; we are running to the future.*[29]
>
> (Translated by the Author)

These lyrics delivered the theme of the Seventh National Games: an open China awaits the 2000 Olympics, and they express Chinese people's hope to merge into the world. It was popular among Chinese audiences, especially the younger generation.[30] In many schools in China, this theme song was selected as the class song and was sung at some school events.[31]

Ceremonies of the National Games

Susan Brownell has pointed out that the opening ceremony attracted the largest single audience among all Olympic events.[32] Similar to the Olympic Games, the ceremonies of the National Games also attracted a large number of Chinese viewers inside and outside the sports stadiums in China. The Chinese government seized the ceremonies of the National Games as a tactical opportunity to disseminate its political ideologies. For example, the ceremonies of the Seventh National Games in 1993 have become more ritualized and regulated to manifest China's capability to host the Olympic Games and to better prepare for the bidding of the 2000 Olympic Games.

In order to 'sell' a national image to a global audience and to prepare for China's Olympic bid, the Organizing Committee invited the IOC president and other members of the IOC to attend the ceremonies of the National Games in China. The IOC president, Juan Antonio Samaranch, was invited to attend the opening ceremonies of the National Games in both 1983 and 1997. The IOC president, Count Jacques Rogge, and other IOC members, were invited to attend the opening ceremonies of the National Games in 2001, 2005 and 2009. By doing so, the Chinese government attempted to use the National Games as evidence to display China's ability to host the Olympic Games and to further showcase the progress of Chinese sport. After watching the 10th National Games in 2005, Rogge said to Liu Peng, the director of the GASC:

> I know the importance of the National Games in China, and it is not only for the athletes but for the whole nation. There is no doubt that after the great success you have achieved in Athens last year during the

Olympic Games, and with the preparations that you have had now for the National Games, I would not be surprised if China would lead the medal count in 2008 Beijing Olympic Games. . . . I am looking forward to seeing the National Games, which are always of the high quality. I remember very well the opening ceremony in Guangzhou four years ago and I expect something that is very, very spectacular.[33]

In addition to attending the ceremonies of the National Games, members of the international sports organizations were also invited to experience traditional Chinese culture and be made aware of China's progress after the pragmatic economic reform and opening-up. Chinese state leaders also utilized their speeches at the ceremonies of the National Games to stress China's capacity to host the Olympic Games.

Olympic medals and the National Games

In cooperation with the Olympic Strategy, the National Games was linked to a new quest for national power and glory in the international sports arena. The achievement of the National Games was not only an indication of China's confidence as a member of the family of world sport but also a manifestation of the Chinese nation's aspiration for a modern, powerful and developed nation-state.

In this period, Chinese elite athletes achieved outstanding performances at the National Games with the support of the 'elite sport is the priority' system and JuguoTizhi. China's progress in elite sports performance has been reflected at every National Games. Many elite athletes were selected at the National Games for the upcoming Olympic Games. For example, Xu Haifeng from the Anhui Province was selected at the Fifth National Games in 1983, and he became China's first Olympic gold medal winner with 566 points in the 60 shots free pistol slow shooting at the 23rd Olympic Games in 1984.[34] Other world champion athletes also earned experience at the National Games and were selected as members of the Chinese sports delegation to compete at the Olympic Games, including gymnast Li Ning, table tennis player Deng Yaping, long-distance runner Wang Junxia, diver Fu Mingxia and basketballer Yao Ming. Liu Xiang was a world record-holder, world champion and Olympic champion in the 110-metre hurdles. Simultaneously, he was also one of China's most successful athletes and a national icon. Liu Xiang's attendance and victory at three National Games in 2001, 2005 and 2009 turned the sports arenas for track and field into the most favourable sites for Chinese spectators. These superstars at the National Games were regarded as 'the Pride of China and the hope of Chinese people' or 'national heroes' that inspired the Chinese nation.[35]

Moreover, the National Games provided an effective experience for the future staging of other international mega-sports events, such as the 1990 Asian Games in Beijing, the 26th Shenzhen Summer Universiade in 2001 and the 2008 Olympic Games.

The National Games, commercialization and drug abuse

After Deng Xiaoping's implementation of economic reform and decentralization, China's sports system was encouraged to stand on its own feet rather than rely on government subsidies.[36] The Chinese government provided more freedom to develop sports commercialization. The Olympics' marketing experience also motivated the Organizing Committee to turn the National Games into a profitable enterprise via sponsorship, the selling of copyrights and usage rights of the mascot, emblem and theme song; issuing lottery tickets; organizing tour groups and marketing the sports stadiums and arenas (see Figure 4.1). The further commercialization of the games in recent years – the advertising as well as corporation sponsorship – provided more funding for the running of the games.

However, the commercialization of the National Games, which occurred in tandem with the commercialization of the Olympic Games, was perceived by many scholars as devaluing the spirit or purpose for which the games were originally established.[37] The commercialization of more recent National Games in China was also criticized by some sports experts and scholars because it had some negative effects on the games.

Figure 4.1 Emblems and Mascots of the Fifth to 11th National Games in the PRC

Source: 'The former National Games', *The official website of the 12th National Games*, Last modified July 14, 2014, www.liaoning2013.com.cn/lijie_new/.

Harvey has concluded that after the transformation from a central government to the more comparative autonomy of local government, the competition to host and manage mega-sports events became an integral part of urban politics.[38] After the local or regional government's bidding to host a sports event, the covering cost and supportive infrastructure of the sports event, along with the staging of it, became significant to the local or regional government.[39] It was also claimed that

> politicians who are involved in the organization of prestigious sports events, such as the Olympics, have the opportunity to improve their political image by associating themselves with the event, as well as to develop their public relations through contacts with sporting authorities and commercial organizations involved in the event.[40]

After the implementation of the bidding system of the National Games in China, the games became part of urban politics, too.

To fulfil the Olympic Strategy, the Chinese central government encouraged all local provincial governments to train and select more athletes for the Olympic Games because sporting success had been historically and socially important to China. At the same time, the successful staging of the National Games, or the athletes' performance, became a way to evaluate the achievements of local dignitaries. To some extent, interprovincial competition became intensified, and the National Games became a central stage for demonstrating physical excellence and regional identities in China. Local governments, especially the host province, formulated their *National Games Strategy* to win more medals and concentrated overwhelmingly on rankings at the National Games. The main reason for this was that elite sport could provide more obvious criteria to evaluate local sports officials' abilities and promotional opportunities.[41] Thus, the National Games even got a nickname: the Authorities Pride Games due to the fierce competition from local sports officials from different provinces and sport associations to preserve their reputations.[42]

To win more medals, the provincial government focused on developing some sports events rather than prioritizing the Olympic Strategy, although China has formulated several regulations to benefit the local provinces. Firstly, the majority of the local provincial governments spent less funds on some sports events that were traditionally strong sports events of other provinces. For example, basketball had become the dominant event for Beijing, Guangdong and the PLA in the history of the National Games in the PRC. Liu Xiang from Shanghai, the world champion and Olympic champion for the men's 110-metres hurdles, was the absolute gold medal winner.[43] This meant that other provinces would not spend too much on the development of these sports events because the chance of getting a gold medal was remote. This resulted in unbalanced sports development in different regions in China. Secondly, the initial purpose of the Athletes Exchange Policy was to give more opportunities to athletes with similar performance to compete and to help select elite athletes for competing at the Olympic Games. However, the exchange policy regarding athletes at the National Games became a shortcut to winning more medals among different provinces, especially the host province, and they improved the bonus money to attract more top athletes to compete for them. The Shandong province, for instance, spent three million Yuan to invite top-level Inner Mongolia basketball player Bate'er to be a member of the Shandong Basketball Team in 2009.[44] Thus, the National Games has on occasion been known as 'the Money Games' in this commercialized society (see Figure 4.2).

This clearly shows that some provinces were willing to spend a large amount of money to win more medals at the National Games. Victory at the National Games became one of the most visible inducements for local sports officials and became interlinked with their future prospects. Additionally, athletes and their coaches also favoured to represent whichever provincial government promised the most bonus money or other profits.

The abuse of drugs has also been an increasing issue at the National Games. For example, at the 10th National Games, Sun Yingjie, a leading Chinese female long-distance runner, tested positive for Androsterone,

Figure 4.2 Expense of the Buying and Selling of Athletes for Gold Medals at the National Games

Source: Tao Zhang, 'The National Games: Athletes Trafficking Communication', *Wangyi Sport*, September 11, 2013, accessed March 19, 2015, http://sports.163.com/special/anglezero/qyrfz.html.

a banned substance, after the games.[45] An investigation followed as Sun claimed she was framed by the other athlete, but she was still fined 10,000 RMB and banned from attending competitions for two years, and her coach was banned for life.[46] In line with the 'zero-tolerance' attitude toward doping offences of the national sports authority in China, every Organizing Committee of the National Games put forward its own anti-doping policy. However, some athletes still took shortcuts by using drugs. For example, at the 11th National Games in 2009, Guo Linna (a rower from the Henan province) and Li Jie (a shooter from Inner Mongolia) tested positive for banned drugs. Twenty-one-year-old sprinter Wang Jing won a gold medal at the women's 100-metre final, but she then tested positive for banned drugs and was disqualified.[47] The National Games was ironically regarded as 'the Drug Games' by many Chinese netizens.[48] Most provincial officials only paid lip service to it. They did not overtly or directly involve in the discreditable drug abuse, yet it was likely that they only kept 'one eye open and one shut'.[49]

At various times the National Games have been referred to as the 'Authorities Pride Games', the 'Money Games', or the 'Drug Games' by different media sphere. The unhealthy development of the National Games in China has been criticized by many experts and the general public since the National Games has been a vehicle for officials, coaches and athletes to further their careers and gain both fame and wealth.[50] Many Chinese academics and administrators in sports authorities publicly questioned whether the National Games should continue, and whether the promotion of mass sport at the grassroots level should take precedence over funding to stage the National Games.[51]

Despite the controversies and scandals of the National Games, the games have always contributed to China's performance at the Olympic Games and have continuously been utilized as a spotlight to demonstrate China's national unity via the dissemination of the mass media, especially via the new media with China's transformation of telecommunication in the globalization context.[52]

The National Games and the media

These National Games were clearly of considerable contemporary importance for China and the Chinese people. They attracted the attention of the nation's leaders, they absorbed a good deal of the nation's resources, they captured a large audience, and they were among the most visible representations of the Chinese nation. The latter was particularly important since these games could well be compared with education in terms of the creation of Benedict Anderson's 'imagined community'.[53] Contrary to Susan

Brownell's statement on the Olympic Games that contributed towards 'the formation of a trans-national community that helps to form global public opinion',[54] the National Games in China was a national gathering to demonstrate national unity. The grand sports stadium allowed thousands of spectators to watch and experience the games in person. This included state leaders, coaches, athletes and referees, as well as a large number of participants from universities and communities. They shared their experiences and comments on the games to their family members or friends, which expanded the common experiences for the imagined Chinese community.

The relationship between sports events and the mass media has been on the public agenda since the growth of television since the 1960s. The significance of television for sport, in terms of its economic and cultural impact, has been a key issue in many countries.[55] Kenneth Roberts stated that sports events have the ability to transmit promotional messages to billions of people via television and other developments in telecommunication.[56] Sports events, as interaction rituals, focused people's attention on national symbols in a manner designed to invoke their loyalty.[57] Garry Whannel argued that 'media representations of sport inevitably involve the production of images of national identities'.[58] It is clear that mass media has played a crucial role in mediating between people and strengthening people's collective national consciousness.

From 1959 to 1979, the National Games benefited from China's state-run media system, which represented the Chinese state in a positive way and was geared towards the construction of Chinese national identity at the grassroots level. Despite these newspaper and radio media, the rapid expansion of the television system has brought state news into the majority of Chinese people's living rooms since the 1980s. The state-run China Central Television (CCTV) was also relayed by many regional television stations. In 1983, the 11th Chinese Radio and Television Conference was held, and the conference concluded with the formulation of policies on the functions of radio and television:

> Radio and television are the most powerful modern tools in encouraging the people of the nation to strive to create a socialist civilization that is both materially and culturally rich. They are the most effective connections between the CCP, the Chinese government and the Chinese people.[59]

As a result of this conference, the Chinese government ratified a policy to encourage the further development of the Chinese television system. Thus, the number of television stations increased from 52 in 1983 to 422 by the end of 1988. Since then, more transmitting stations and relay stations have been established by the state and local governments.[60] In addition, Chinese ownership of television sets increased and, by the end of the 1990s, most urban Chinese families had television sets.[61] China's television penetration rate has been increasingly improved with the booming free market; in the 2000s the majority of the population in urban and rural China has access to television. Thus, television plays a more important role in Chinese people's daily life, providing them with news, education and entertainment. The influence of television on the dissemination of the National Games is likely to be much greater than that of any other mass medium in China now.

In the 1980s, the National Games were broadcasted by both the CCTV and some regional and local television stations in Shanghai, Guangzhou, Tianjin, Shanxi, Zhejiang and Jiangsu.[62] Television sports coverage in China had large audiences in the 1990s, and television became a way for (predominantly urban) Chinese people to view major international and national sports events. In fact, CCTV and local television stations broadcast more than 800 hours of the Seventh and Eighth National Games, especially the ceremonies of the games and the finals.[63] In 1995, CCTV established a channel for sport: CCTV-5, which was the first channel exclusively dedicated to sport in China.[64] CCTV-5 shouldered the broadcasting of most of the national and international mega-sports events in China, including the National Games.

In this period, the language of the broadcasting of the National Games was filled with repetitive phrases, including 'Motherland', 'Chinese nation', 'Chinese anthem', 'Five-starred Red Flag', 'Chinese national heroes', 'Win national glory', 'Ode to the motherland' and 'Honor belongs to the motherland'. In addition, the television station had a strong visual impact so that the animated speeches from state leaders and the rituals full of Chinese national symbols at the National Games' stadia could be directly disseminated to those viewers who were not physically present.

From the Ninth National Games in 2001, the Organizing Committee sold the broadcasting rights of the games to CCTV and other television stations; meanwhile, the official sponsorship of the National Games also gave the Organizing Committee the funds to facilitate the National Games because, as part of the deal, the commercial advertisements of their products were interrupted by broadcasts from the National Games. Despite being a political propaganda tool for the Chinese government, the mass media also generated funds for the games and benefited the sponsors of the games in a more market-oriented economic system.

Despite the commercialization of the television broadcasting rights of the National Games, the popularity of satellite TV and the Internet has revolutionized the way in which popular audiences all over China view the National Games. This caused an expansion of the audiences for the games, especially due to the Internet, which enabled the National Games in China to cross borders and conveyed information on a global scale. An increasing number of people, both inside and outside China, had access to the National Games via digital television, Internet and mobile devices.

The same mass rituals were shared among the Chinese people via the mass media, which helped the Chinese people to develop a sense of belonging to the Chinese nation and to realize Benedict Anderson's notion of 'imagined communities'.[65] For instance, since the Ninth National Games in 2001, each of the Organizing Committees designed its own official website to broadcast the games and to bolster Chinese common memories. The official website of the GSAC, the COC, China.com (it belongs to China Radio International) and other web portals also provided the latest news about the National Games.[66] In addition, international media outlets were also involved in the reporting of the National Games, which allowed overseas Chinese to share the same information with other members within China. For example, some of the recent sport competitions and ceremonies of the National Games could be watched on YouTube.

It also became easier for the public to comment on the National Games and share their comments with others on the Internet. Although the Chinese government had blocked access to YouTube, Facebook and Twitter to avoid potential political protests facilitated by social media after riots by ethnic Uyghur in Xinjiang province in 2009,[67] some Chinese Bulletin Board System (BBS) forums or web chat tools, such as Tianya, Sina blog, microblog and Tencent's QQ, were designed as hugely popular micro-blogging platforms. They allowed interactive communications among people across regional boundaries within China, or even across national boundaries in the world.[68]

In addition, the state-run media and other local media have made huge efforts to encourage the devotion of young people to the development of Chinese society by advertising for volunteers at the National Games. The hosting of the National Games has involved thousands of volunteer citizens or students. Volunteers at the 10th National Games in 2005 also provided valuable experience for the 2008 Olympic Games. One of the respondents talked about his personal experience as a volunteer for the 11th National Games in 2009:[69]

> Volunteering does not seem to be an easy commitment, but I felt so proud when I devoted myself to my beloved motherland. . . . As a sophomore, I also benefited a lot from the volunteering. Athletes' fighting spirit at the National Games and the Olympic Games encouraged me to be much stronger mentally and physically. I became more confident in communicating with diverse people and develop my sociability. It also helped me to see a different way of life.[70]

Stories and pictures of the young students like this one who did their volunteering services at the sports arenas were repeatedly broadcast by the mass media.[71] Thus, the mass media, to a certain degree, acted as a surrogate venue for eliciting voluntary patriotism from the younger generation via serving the National Games.

National Games, nationalism and globalization

Since the 1980s the change of policy priority in China did not indicate the diminishing of Chinese nationalism, but a transformation of Chinese state-led nationalism from anti-imperialist or anti-traditional nationalism to a more pragmatic and flexible attitude towards nationalism for economic development and national revival. Chinese pragmatic nationalism was 'national interest-driven', and its main objective was to 'build a politically, economically, and culturally united nation-state when foreign and largely Western influences are seen as eroding the nation-state's very foundation.'[72] Thus, the economic modernization and improvement of the Chinese people's living standards have become the central tasks of the Chinese government since the 1980s. Pragmatic nationalism insisted that the universal culture be subject to the promotion of Chinese national interests or the enhancement of national pride. It was more critical of any imported universal principles, including Marxism, emphasized the gap between Western models and Chinese conditions and stressed its political ideology of 'socialism with Chinese characteristics'.[73]

Since the 1980s, the Chinese government implemented Deng Xiaoping's reform and opening-up policy to develop the national economy, to improve Chinese people's living standards and to realize the goal of modernization. China actively opened its door to become involved in the process of globalization.

Giddens claims that globalization 'refers to that stretching process, in so far as the modes of connection between different social contexts or regions become networked across the earth's surface as a whole'.[74] That is to say, globalization is a process, and this process has its influence on societies, cultures, and nations in most parts of the world. China was eager to be a member of the global community through trade, investment and technological transfer to achieve its economic modernization; meanwhile, China took an opening-up attitude towards Western culture and ideas, including Western sport.

Houlihan suggested that 'globalization, as related to sport, is . . . most evident and significant in providing governments with a further medium through which to conduct international politics'.[75] China's return to the IOC and subsequently to other international sports federations marked the beginning of China's global communication and interaction in sport. It also indicated that Chinese sport was entering a new era where the political role of Chinese sport now rested squarely on the shoulders of the nation's performance at the Olympic Games and the world champions. Since the 1980s, China reformed its sports policy from an emphasis on *friendship through sport* to *winning gold medals* at international sports events. The excellent performances of Chinese athletes in international sports arenas 'were indicative of China's other achievements in the areas of economic reform and modernization'.[76] The number of gold medals, in particular Olympic gold medals, was linked to China's international prestige, the ideology of patriotism as well as the superiority of socialism with Chinese characteristics. China's two bids for the Olympic Games were also highly political and illustrated that the Chinese government had put much effort into raising Chinese national pride and strengthening the cohesion of Chinese people and society through the Olympic Games.[77]

In response to the requirement of China's Olympic Strategy and the increasing sports commercialization and globalization, the National Games experienced a continuous transformation. This was also reflected in the rising of a Chinese state-led pragmatic nationalism for national revival in the area of sports development in China.

Firstly, the National Games became a 'training and testing ground' to get Chinese athletes ready for the Olympic Games because the Olympic success of Chinese athletes was a political statement to showcase Chinese national pride and international prestige, economic development as well as political superiority. From the Fifth National Games in 1983, the reformation of the National Games was in line with the Olympic Games, so it could be argued that the reformation of the National Games was mainly Olympic-directed. The National Games has even been called the 'mini-Olympic Games' in China.[78] For example, most competitive sports events at the National Games were the same as those in the forthcoming Olympic Games, which coincided with China's sports principle of 'Train the athletes at home and compete against the foreign competitors' as well as the pattern of being in line with the format of the Olympic Games. In order to support China's ambition for the bidding of the 2000 Olympic Games, the Seventh National Games changed its scheduled host city from Chengdu in Sichuan province to Beijing to utilize the National Games as a window to display China's ability to stage the Olympic Games. The Organizing Committee of the National Games also invited many IOC members as guests to the National Games to demonstrate China's capabilities. Moreover, the 10th National Games in 2005 played a direct and pivotal role in the successful running of the 2008 Beijing Olympic Games. Hence, the National Games assisted the increase in China's Olympic gold-medal ranking.

Secondly, the Chinese government adopted an IOC model of marketization and commercialization of sports events to run and support the National Games. This led to a gradual decentralization and commercialization of the National Games in which the Games partly realized its own financial independence. The commercialization of the National Games in China also illustrated China's shifting political focus since the 1980s from class struggle to economic development for modernization. The Organizing Committee of the National Games encouraged state-run and private enterprises as well as foreign corporations to invest in the games and/or provide sponsorship for sports delegations or teams to raise money to achieve its objective of autonomy rather than reliance on government budget. The commercialization and marketization of the National Games, including the sponsorships, partnerships, lottery and the sale of broadcasting rights, helped relieve the financial and administrative burden on the Chinese central government. However, the increase in the pursuit of winning medals and the growth of commercialization also led to an increase of controversial issues and scandals at the National Games, such as drug abuse and corruption.

In addition, the globalization of information and communications technology also provided more ways to promote the National Games. With the diversified media technology, the National Games captured a very large audience via television and the Internet. The National Games was still among the most visible representations of the Chinese nation, such as performances at the ceremonies of the Games, which reflected the social progress and sustainable development of China. The grand sports stadium itself and the media reports allowed thousands of spectators to experience the games in person or at home. Through watching the National Games, an increased chance to develop the common experiences and memories was created for the Chinese people in the imagined Chinese community. Hence, the National Games continued to be a national gathering to demonstrate national unity and national identity.

Notes

1 Anthony Giddens, *The Consequences of Modernity* (Cambridge: Polity, 1990), 225.
2 Robert J. Holton, *Globalization and the Nation State* (New York: Palgrave Macmillan, 2011), 2.
3 Hsu, *Rise of Modern China*, 841.
4 Rozman Gilbert, ed., *The Modernization of China* (New York: Simon and Schuster, 1982), 471–473.
5 Zhao, 'Chinese Nationalism and Its International Orientations', 1–33.
6 Lowell Dittmer and Guoli Liu, eds., *China's Deep Reform: Domestic Politics in Transition* (New York: Rowman & Littlefield Publishers), 2006.

7 Tien-Chin Tan, 'Chinese Sports Policy and Globalization: The Case of the Olympic Movement, Elite Football and Elite Basketball' (PhD thesis, Loughborough University, Leicestershire, UK, 2008), 145.
8 Hong Fan, 'Into the Future: Asian Sport and Globalization', in James A. Mangan and Hong Fan, eds., *Sport in Asian Society: Past and Present* (London: Frank Cass, 2003): 402–404.
9 Xu, *Olympic Dreams*, 197–198.
10 Ibid.
11 Ibid., 203.
12 Hong Fan, Duncan Mackay and Karen Christensen, eds., *China Gold: China's Quest for Global Power and Olympic Glory* (Great Barrington: Berkshire Publishing Group, 2008), 99–103.
13 Ibid., 99–103.
14 Christopher R. Hill, *Olympic Politics* (Manchester: Manchester University Press, 1996), 31; Brownell, *Training the Body for China*, 314.
15 Brownell, *Training the Body for China*, 110.
16 The GASC, *Yearbook of the Sport in China (1996)* (Beijing: People's Sport Press, 1999), 159–161.
17 'An Outline of the National Fitness Program of China', *The Official Website of the COC*, June 8, 2005, accessed February 28, 2015, http://en.olympic.cn/sport_for/nfp_project/2005-06-08/121888.html.
18 Allen Guttmann, *Games and Empires: Modern Sports and Cultural Imperialism* (New York: Columbia University Press, 1994), 164.
19 Hao Qin, ed., *Sports History in China, 1980–1992* (Beijing: People's Sport Press, 2008), 96–99.
20 'The 7th National Games: Beijing/Sichuan 1993', *The Official Website of the COC*, March 27, 2004, accessed July 8, 2014, http://en.olympic.cn/games/national/2004-03-27/121778.html.
21 Jianhui Zhang, *The Transformation of the Institution of the National Games: Order, Identity, and Profit* (Beijing: Beijing Sport University Press, 2011), 131
22 'The Chinese Olympic Dream Has Come True', *Xinhua News*, July 14, 2001.
23 From interview material in China.
24 Shouhe Cao, ed., *The History of Sport in China* (Beijing: People's Sport Press, 2008), 324–325.
25 Jianhui Zhang, 'The 60 Years Evolution of National Games Institution 1949–2009', *China Sport Science and Technology* 48, no. 2 (2012): 16–17.
26 Yu Tao, 'Research on the Impact of Holding the National Games in a Variety of Cities – a Case of the 10th National Games', *The Official Website of the GASC*, May 5, 2009, accessed March 10, 2015, www.sport.gov.cn/n16/n1152/n2523/n377568/n377613/n377808/1100688.html.
27 Weimin Yuan, ed., *China Sport Yearbook 2007* (Beijing: China Sport Yearbook Press, 2000), 151.
28 'The Former National Games', *The Official Website of the 12th National Games*, Last modified July 14, 2014, www.liaoning2013.com.cn/lijie_new/.
29 The GASC, *The 10 National Games of China*, 135.
30 From interview material in China.
31 Ibid.
32 Susan Brownell, 'The Olympic Public Sphere: The London and Beijing Opening Ceremonies as Representative of Political Systems', *The International Journal of the History of Sport* 30, no. 11 (2013): 1315–1327.

33 'IOC President Raves about China's National Games', *JiangsuNews (English)*, October 18, 2005, accessed 16 March 2015, http://english.jschina.com.cn/special/english/25784/25796/201408/t1538738.shtml.

34 The GASC, *The 10th National Games of China* (Beijing: People's Sports Publishing House of China, 2006), 90–92.

35 Xiangguang Chen, 'Chinese Sport Stars' Impacts to Chinese College Students and Humanistic Education', *Journal of Physical Education* 13, no. 4 (2006): 15–18.

36 Wei Fan, Hong Fan and Zhouxiang Lu, 'Chinese State Sports Policy: Pre- and Post-Beijing 2008', *The International Journal of the History of Sport* 27, nos. 14–15 (2010): 2380–2402.

37 Holger Preuss, *The Economics of Staging the Olympics: A Comparison of the Games, 1972–2008* (Northampton, MA: Edward Elgar Publishing, 2004); Alan Tomlinson, 'The Commercialization of the Olympics: Cities, Corporations and the Olympic Commodity', *Global Olympics: Historical and Sociological Studies of the Modern Games* 3 (2005): 179.

38 David Harvey, *The Urban Experience* (Baltimore: Johns Hopkins University Press, 1989), 23–25.

39 Malfas Maximos, Barrie Houlihan and Eleni Theodoraki, 'Impacts of the Olympic Games as Mega-Events, in the ICE', *Municipal Engineer* 157, no. 3 (2004): 215–216.

40 Ibid., 217.

41 Xiaochen Sun, 'National Games in Dire Need of Reform', *China Daily*, September 7, 2013, accessed March 18, 2015, http://usa.chinadaily.com.cn/china/2013-09/07/content_16950908.htm.

42 Jessie, 'China 11th National Games: Controversies, Scandals, Costs', *ChinaSMACK*, October 29, 2009, accessed March 19, 2015, www.chinasmack.com/2009/stories/11th-national-games-controversies-scandals-costs.html.

43 In the 12 times of the National Games in the PRC until 2015, the PLA has won the men's basketball championship 7 times and Beijing and Guangdong have won the men's basketball championship twice respectively. Liu Xiang attended the 9th, 10th and 11th National Games and won three championships at the men's 110-metre hurdles. Statistics from the official website of the GASC, accessed at www.sport.gov.cn/n16/n1122/n1983/n32333/index.html.

44 He Zhai, 'BaTe'er Signed a Contract with Liaoning for the National Games and He Got 2 Million RMB and a 1.4 Million RMB House', *Sohu Sport*, February 27, 2012, accessed April 24, 2015, http://sports.sohu.com/20120227/n335996494.shtml.

45 Wei Sun, 'The View of Life of Human Beings in Competitive Sport', *Journal of Physical Education* 14, no. 8 (2007): 21–23.

46 Ming Yang, 'If Sun Yingjie Were Not be Framed', *Xinhua Daily Telegraph*, December 19, 2005, 3.

47 'Doping Sprinter Claims Setup', *Sina English*, October 28, 2009, accessed May 12, 2015, http://english.sina.com/sports/p/2009/1027/280941.html.

48 Hua Yang, 'Has the National Games Got Rid of the Drugs', *DagongBao (大公报)*, September 13, 2013, 8.

49 From interview material in China.

50 Ibid.

51 Ibid.

52 New media commonly referred to content available on-demand through the Internet and the interplay between technology, images and sound, accessible

on a digital device, usually containing interactive user feedback and creative participation, which enabled people around the world to share, comment on and discuss a wide variety of topics. The new media included websites such as online newspapers and videos, blogs, micro-blogs, or other social media. Bailey Socha and Barbara Eber-Schmid, 'What Is New Media? Defining New Media Isn't Easy', *The New Media Institution*, accessed March 19, 2015, www.new media.org/what-is-new-media.html.

53 Anderson, *Imagined Communities*.

54 Brownell, 'The Olympic Public Sphere', 1315–1327.

55 Urbain Claeys and Herman V. Pelt, 'Sport and the Mass Media: Like Bacon and Eggs', *International Review for the Sociology of Sport* 21, nos. 2–3 (1986): 95–101. Robert W. McChesney, 'Media Made Sport: A History of Sports Coverage in the United States', *Media, Sports, and Society* (1989): 49–69.

56 Roberts Kenneth, *The Leisure Industries* (New York: Palgrave Macmillan, 2004).

57 Hargreaves, *Sport, Power and Culture*, 12.

58 Garry Whannel, 'Sport and the Media', in Jay Coakley and Eric Dunning, eds., *Handbook of Sport Studies* (Thousand Oaks, CA: Sage, 2000): 300.

59 Editor, *China Today: Radio and Television* (Beijing: Chinese Social Science Press, 1987), 45.

60 Xiaoping Li, 'The Chinese Television System and Television News', *The China Quarterly* 126 (1991): 340–355.

61 National Bureau of Statistics of China, *Special Report: China Statistics 1990* (Beijing: China's Statistics Press, 1991), 213–217.

62 Hepu Li, 'The 6th National Games Will Be Opened at City of Goat-Guangzhou', *Journal of Liaowang* 46, no. 9 (1987): 24–25.

63 Desheng Zhang, 'Research on the Development Tendency of China's Sport Media Communication', *Journal of Wuhan Sport Institute* 44, no. 7 (2010): 16–19.

64 Qingjun Wang, 'Contemplation of Traditional Sport Going into Media in China-taking "Wulin Assembly" on CCTV-5 for Example', *Journal of Physical Education* 16, no. 4 (2009): 90–92.

65 Anderson, *Imagined Communities*, 37–46.

66 The Subject on the National Games in the PRC Can Be Searched from the Website, Such as, http://en.olympic.cn/games/national/ & www.sport.gov.cn/n16/n1122/n1983/n32333/index.html&.

67 Brownell, 'The Olympic Public Sphere', 1315–1327.

68 Sina's Weibo, Tencent's QQ and Wechat borrowed some features from both Facebook and Twitter, but in China they are maintained by the Chinese Censorship of the Internet, which is conducted under a wide variety of laws and administrative regulations by the Chinese central government. Xueyang Xu, Morley Z. Mao and Alex J. Halderman, 'Internet Censorship in China: Where Does the Filtering Occur?', in Gerhard Goos, ed., *Passive and Active Measurement 2011* (Berlin: Springer Berlin Heidelberg, 2011): 133–142.

69 As one of the volunteer students in the 2009 Asian Grand Prix, Suzhou, the author herself have similar feelings and experiences as he did when both of us were college students.

70 From interview material in China.

71 Wenwen Guo, ed., 'The National Games Volunteer Guo Peng: Everybody Is Not Easy', *Xinhuanet*, July 31, 2013, accessed March 21, 2015, www.liaoning2013.com.cn/system/2013/07/31/010596295.shtml.

72 Jisi Wang, 'Pragmatic Nationalism: China Seeks a New Role in World Affairs', *Oxford International Review* 6, no. 1 (1994): 28–30.
73 Zhao, 'Chinese Nationalism and Its International Orientations', 1–33.
74 Giddens, *The Consequence of Modernity*, 64.
75 Barrie Houlihan, *Sport and International Politics* (Hemel Hempstead, UK: Harvester Wheatsheaf, 1994), 200–201.
76 Lu and Fan, *Sport and Nationalism in China*, 102.
77 Xu, *Olympic Dreams*; Zhao, 'The Olympics and Chinese Nationalism', 48–57.
78 From interview material in China.

References

Alan, Tomlinson. 'The Commercialization of the Olympics: Cities, Corporations and the Olympic Commodity.' *Global Olympics: Historical and Sociological Studies of the Modern Games* 3 (2005): 179–200.

Anderson, Benedict. *Imagined Communities: Reflections on the Origin and Spread of Nationalism*. London: Verso Books, 2006.

Brownell, Susan. 'The Olympic Public Sphere: The London and Beijing Opening Ceremonies as Representative of Political Systems.' *The International Journal of the History of Sport* 30, no. 11 (2013): 1315–1327.

Brownell, Susan. *Training the Body for China: Sports in the Moral Order of the People's Republic*. Chicago: University of Chicago Press, 1995.

Claeys, Urbain, and Herman V. Pelt. 'Sport and the Mass Media: Like Bacon and Eggs.' *International Review for the Sociology of Sport* 21, nos. 2–3 (1986): 95–101.

Dittmer, Lowell, and Liu, Guoli, eds. *China's Deep Reform: Domestic Politics in Transition*. New York: Rowman & Littlefield Publishers, 2006.

Fan, Hong, Duncan Mackay, and Karen Christensen, eds. *China Gold: China's Quest for Global Power and Olympic Glory*. Great Barrington: Berkshire Publishing Group, 2008.

Fan, Hong. 'Into the Future: Asian Sport and Globalization.' In *Sport in Asian Society: Past and Present*, edited by James A. Mangan and Hong Fan, 402–404. London and Portland, OR: Frank Cass, 2003.

The GASC. *The 10th National Games of China*. Beijing: People's Sports Publishing House of China, 2006.

The GASC. *Yearbook of the Sport in China (1996)*. Beijing: People's Sport Press, 1999.

Giddens, Anthony. *The Consequences of Modernity*. Cambridge: Polity, 1990.

Gilbert, Rozman, ed. *The Modernization of China*. New York: Simon and Schuster, 1982.

Guttmann, Allen. *Games and Empires: Modern Sports and Cultural Imperialism*. New York: Columbia University Press, 1994.

Harvey, David. *The Urban Experience*. Baltimore: Johns Hopkins University Press, 1989.

Hill, Christopher R. *Olympic Politics*. Manchester: Manchester University Press, 1996.

Holton, Robert J. *Globalization and the Nation State*. New York: Palgrave Macmillan, 2011.

Houlihan, Barrie. *Sport and International Politics*. Hemel Hempstead, UK: Harvester Wheatsheaf, 1994.

Kenneth, Roberts. *The Leisure Industries*. New York: Palgrave Macmillan, 2004.

Lu, Zhouxiang, and Hong Fan. *Sport and Nationalism in China*. London and New York: Routledge, 2013.

Malfas, Maximos, Barrie Houlihan, and Eleni Theodoraki. 'Impacts of the Olympic Games as Mega – Events in the ICE.' *Municipal Engineer* 157, no. 3 (2004): 209–220.

Qin, Hao, ed. *Sports History in China, 1980–1992*. Beijing: People's Sport Press, 2008.

Tan, Tien-Chin. 'Chinese Sports Policy and Globalization: The Case of the Olympic Movement, Elite Football and Elite Basketball.' Ph.D., Loughborough University, Leicestershire, UK, 2008.

Whannel, Garry. 'Sport and the Media.' In *Handbook of Sport Studies*, edited by Jay Coakley and Eric Dunning, 291–308. Thousand Oaks, CA: Sage, 2000.

Xu, Guoqi. *Olympic Dreams: China and Sports, 1895–2008*. Cambridge, MA: Harvard University Press, 2009.

Yuan, Weimin, ed. *China Sport Yearbook 2007*. Beijing: China Sport Yearbook Press, 2000.

Zhao, Suisheng. 'The Olympics and Chinese Nationalism.' *China Security* 4, no. 3 (2008): 48–57.

Zhao, Suisheng. 'Chinese Nationalism and Its International Orientations.' *Political Science Quarterly* 115, no. 1 (2000): 1–33.

5 The National Games and national identity in China

Since the turn of the 19th century, modern Chinese sport has contributed to the creation of a new modern Chinese nation-state by means of the values of competition, sportsmanship, self-confidence, awareness and discipline.[1] The introduction of Western sport to Chinese society in the late Qing Dynasty has been integral to the process of Chinese nation building. The YMCA in China played a vital role in the development of the National Games in China. Under the YMCA's leadership, the first two National Games in China were held in Nanjing in 1910 and Beijing in 1914. The athletes who competed at these two Games were predominantly Chinese students from different regions of China. The majority of the referees for these two Games were Westerners from the YMCA in China. The official language of the Games was English.

The spectators of these two Games were privileged college students at the time. Most Chinese had never heard of the National Games. Therefore, arguably, the birth of the National Games in China had nothing to do with Chinese nationalism or Chinese national identity. Rather, this was an overt representation of Western sport together with Western cultural imperialism in China. Nevertheless, the crowning achievement of the YMCA in China was that it planted the seed of China's interest in modern sport. It also paved the way for the Chinese people's determination to reclaim sports sovereignty from Western influence.

Fuelled by the painful history of Western invasions and Chinese anti-imperialist nationalist sentiments, sport was recognized as a resource that could be harnessed to strengthen the nation. The embarrassing lack of ability to host the National Games and to organize the Chinese sports squad to compete at the Olympic Games and the FECGs concerned Chinese nationalists and politicians alike. Chinese nationalists were eager to take back sports sovereignty from the control of the Western imperialists. They valued sport and saw its potential to display the Chinese people's body in order to erase the humiliating title, 'the sick man of East Asia'; through the rituals of sport, Chinese people could be mobilized and their experience consolidated into a collective sense of belonging to the nation and nationhood. Furthermore, the nationalists professed that a national sports event offered the vision of symbolic, participatory and celebratory national community.[2]

Chinese nationalists seized the opportunity to host the Third National Games in 1924, whilst efforts were being made by local sports organizations in the provinces to establish China's first national sports organization: the China National Amateur Athletic Federation (CNAAF). These two events marked the beginning of China's self-governance of its own mega-sports event.[3] With the help of publicity from politicians, scholars and the print media, the Third National Games in 1924 bound people to protect Chinese sovereignty and firmly safeguard the independence of the Chinese nation.

It was recognized by the leading Chinese Nationalists that the National Games played an important role in maintaining nationhood and increasing national cohesion. From 1927 the Nanjing nationalist government gave its support for the development of the National Games. The involvement of the nationalist government was instrumental to the growth of the National Games. From 1930 to 1948 in the Republic of China, the Fourth, Fifth, Sixth and Seventh National Games were guided and financially sponsored by the nationalist government.

Under the nationalist government the National Games served the polity, as the sports arena itself was discovered to be the best mass-media conduit for the promotion of Chinese nationalism, anti-imperialism and patriotism. In particular, while the Northeast was under Japanese control after the Mukden Incident in 1931, the intensity of the competitions as well as the rituals and symbols at the arenas of the 1933 National Games were a platform for reminding the Chinese public that the Northeast region rightly belonged to China. The 10,000 spectators at the opening of the 1933 National Games ceremony shouted to express their shared hope of reclaiming this area from the Japanese. The rituals of the 1933 National Games were deployed to motivate the Chinese citizenry to unite as a national community to proclaim territorial integrity and to protest against the Japanese occupation. Furthermore, the National Games allowed for the development of modern Chinese elite sport and contributed to China's involvement in international sports events such as the FECGs and the Olympic Games in the Republic of China era. Many Chinese athletes who competed at the Olympics were trained and selected at the National Games. Even if Chinese athletes' participation in the Olympic Games in the Republic of China did not lead to the winning of medals, their presence was a turning point for China's use of sport as a means to be visible on the world stage as an independent nation-state equal to the rest of the world.

In addition, the close ties between the National Games and the National Products Movement (1900 to 1937) added a significant economic dimension to the development of Chinese nationalism in sport realm. By promoting the purchase of China's national products or Chinese-made products, as opposed to 'foreign products', the movement offered Chinese people of all classes an opportunity to resist imperialism and express their loyalty to the nation through consumption. In line with this movement, imported sports products at the National Games were gradually replaced by Chinese-made products. Unsurprisingly, the number of sports goods manufacturers in China increased in order to meet the growing demand for sports equipment. With the rising tide of slogans such as 'sport for national salvation' or 'national-products for national salvation', many sports products companies donated products for the National Games to voice patriotism among athletes from different parts of China. Thus, the demand for sports products for the National Games and simultaneously the National Products Movement accelerated the establishment and development of these national sports goods companies and, to a certain extent, maintained Chinese economic and social stability.

Thus, in summary, the birth of the National Games in China was a useful instrument in teaching Chinese people the value of sportsmanship and the form of Western modern sport. More importantly, however, the hosting of the National Games by the Chinese rather than expatriates from the West emphasized the aims of attaining national sovereignty and self-determination. The Nanjing nationalist government grasped the opportunity to utilize this national sports event to promote its political ideologies and to justify the rise of modern China as a legitimate modern nation-state. In a climate of foreign invasions, frequent civil wars, unstable political environment and economic downturn, the seven National Games hosted in the late Qing and the Republican era (1910–1948) could only be regarded as the infant stage of the National Games' development. The hosting of the National Games in the Republican era, however, was consciously identified as being part of a nation-building project for a unified nation-state. The National Games has been shaped by the anti-imperialism and self-defining nationalism that dominated modern Chinese history and also acted as a powerful platform for the development of a sense of national identity and a drive to live in an independent, sovereign nation-state. Thus, the National Games in the Republic of China era was more than a mere sports event, but rather played an important role in shaping Chinese independent nationhood and national identity.

After the establishment of the PRC in 1949, the CCP became the ruling political party of the new regime. Chinese state-led nationalism and communism went side by side as the dominant political ideologies of the state.[4] It did not take long for the new Chinese government to realize the significant political utility of sport in China's nation-building project and in its ambition to improve its international standing and image of the new China. Sport and athletes in China were regarded as having the capacity to transform the 'sick man of East Asia' into a strong and modern nation-state, respected by the rest of the world. In order to implement the objectives of sport in the PRC, the Chinese government established a Soviet model centralized sports system to empower sport with greater international political credibility.

The restoration of the First National Games in the PRC in 1959 was seen as an opportunity to celebrate the 10th anniversary of the new China and to symbolically demonstrate the achievements of the CCP's leadership. Between 1959 and 1979 the State Sports Ministry (SSM) organized the first four National Games in the PRC at irregular intervals in Beijing, the political center of the new regime. These games were supervised and funded by the Chinese government in order that they be regarded as state-led sports events. Compared with the National Games in the period between 1910 and 1948 in the Republic of China, the National Games in the period between 1959 and 1979 gradually formed and developed a well-organized governing and operational system and established a good foundation for future games. Therefore, this period of the first four National Games (1959–1979) could be considered to be a formative stage in the history of its development.

Aside from the development of the ongoing governance and operations of the National Games itself, Chinese nationalism was a continuous incentive behind the games from 1959 to 1979. The National Games was positioned to be a demonstration of the superiority of the socialist system in China. Additionally, the games also reflected the changing focus of Chinese state-led nationalism in this period. For instance, the First National Games in 1959 was not only designed to demonstrate China's 10 years of achievement through communist ideology and China's self-reliance policy, but also mobilized the general public to participate in the games for the purpose of national construction and national defence. Following this, the Second National Games in 1965 both prepared Chinese athletes to attend the GANEFO to challenge Western hegemony in sport and were utilized to publicize the importance of class struggle, socialist revolution and mass military training in preparation for war. Through the nationwide preliminaries and mass calisthenics for the National Games, many military sports events and a militarized training philosophy were popularized in Chinese society.

Moreover, at the Third and the Fourth National Games in 1975 and 1979, the Chinese government tactically established a Taiwan province delegation to stand for national sovereignty and territorial integrity. The state-run news agencies' overstated report on the Taiwanese athletes' desire for reunification illustrated the 1970s Chinese government's political drive for national reunification. In accordance with this, at the National Games ceremonies, athletes from different ethnic groups wearing their own folk costumes evoked the image of China as an inclusive, multicultural nation-state embracing ethnic groups within China's territorial boundaries. This image was also promoted through the Chinese government's national equality and unity policy.

Chinese national symbols, including the PRC's national flag, emblem and anthem, as well as Chairman Mao's portraits, were presented at the Beijing Workers Stadium (the sports stadium for the first four National Games in the PRC) to strengthen the sense of Chinese national identity among its spectators. In this period, thousands of people's performance of mass calisthenics at the ceremonies of the National Games became one of the most effective techniques for inculcating Chinese political commitment to the greater stability and prosperity promised under the CCP's leadership.

In the 1980s, after the decline of Marxism and Chairman Mao's utopian communist vision for the state, Deng Xiaoping launched his more market-oriented economic reforms in China. This was the starting point of Chinese pragmatic nationalism with the goal of achieving modernization.[5] The main objectives of Chinese pragmatic nationalism were to defend, seek out and assert China's national interests by both 'reacting to and absorbing from the outside world'.[6] A number of factors on the domestic front indicated that the Chinese government was now about to take a pragmatic attitude toward nationalism as a value shared between the CCP government and the Chinese people in order to maintain economic modernization and peaceful revitalization of the Chinese nation. These factors have included the market-oriented economic reforms, the CCP government's campaign of patriotic education from the 1990s, as well as the reconstruction of traditional Confucian culture since the 2000s.

On the international front, China's return to the IOC and other international sports federations in 1979 reinforced the relationship between sport and politics and marked the beginning of a new era of sports globalization in China. Sport became a medium for reestablishing contacts with the Western world. Chinese successes at international mega-sports events were regarded by the Chinese government as a form of soft power and an indicator of the rise of 'international prestige, status, and legitimacy'.[7] The sports arena, in other words, became a stage to showcase China's economic and political progress in the post-1980s era. China reformed its sports policies from an initial emphasis on friendship through sport to a focus on winning gold medals in international sporting arenas, in particular the Olympic Games. China's Olympic Strategy was designed in the 1980s to build national pride and pursue international prestige through the Olympic Games. In line with these objectives, the National Games was utilized as a training and testing ground for preparing Chinese athletes for the Olympic Games. Accordingly, many aspects of the National Games from 1983 to 2009 have been reformed in order to be consistent with China's Olympic Strategy. This transformation of the National Games also reflects the push from Chinese state-led pragmatic nationalism for national revival in the area of sports development in China.

Firstly, the National Games became a 'training and testing ground' to get Chinese athletes ready for the Olympic Games, because the Olympic success of Chinese athletes was a political statement, functioning as a showcase of Chinese national pride and international prestige, economic development as well as political superiority. Given that from the Fifth National Games in 1983, the National Games was in line with the Olympic Games, it could be argued that the reformation of the National Games was mainly Olympic-directed. The National Games has even been called the 'mini-Olympic Games' in China.[8] For example, most competitive sports events at the National Games were the same as those in the forthcoming Olympic Games, which coincided with China's sports policy to 'train the athletes at home and compete against the foreign competitors' as well as the pattern of being in line with the format of the Olympic Games. In order to support China's ambition for bidding for the 2000 Olympic Games, the Seventh National Games changed its scheduled host city from Chengdu in Sichuan province to Beijing in order to utilize the National Games as a window to display China's ability to stage the Olympic Games. The Organizing Committee of the National Games also invited many IOC members as guests to the National Games to demonstrate China's capabilities. Moreover, the 10th National Games in 2005 played a direct and pivotal role in the successful running of the 2008 Beijing Olympic Games. The National Games also assisted the increase in China's Olympic gold-medal ranking from fourth place at Los Angeles in 1984 to second at Beijing in 2008.

Secondly, the Chinese government adopted an IOC model of the marketization and commercialization of sports events in order to run and support the National Games. This led to a gradual decentralization and commercialization of the National Games in which the Games partly realized its own financial independence. The commercialization of the National Games in China also illustrated the shifting political focus of China since the 1980s from that of class struggle to that of economic development for the purposes of modernization. The Organizing Committee of the National Games encouraged state-run and private enterprises as well as foreign corporations to invest in the games and/or provide sponsorship for sports delegations or teams to raise money in order to achieve its objective of autonomy rather than reliance on a government budget. The commercialization and marketization of the National Games, including the sponsorships, partnerships, lottery and the sale of broadcasting rights, helped relieve the financial and administrative burden on the Chinese central government. However, the increase in the pursuit of winning medals and the growth of commercial-ization also led to an increasing number of controversies and scandals at the National Games, including drug use, pre-decided gold medals, unfair officiating, match fixing and corruption.

Thirdly, the globalization of information and communications technol-ogy also provided more mechanisms for the promotion of the National Games. With diversified media technology, the National Games captured a very large audience via both television and the Internet. The National Games has been among the most visible representations of the Chinese nation. For example, in accordance with the renewal and reconstruction of traditional culture and beliefs as a mechanism to strengthen the idea of a Chinese nation-state that has been occurring since the 2000s, the opening and closing ceremonies of the 10th and 11th National Games narrated Chi-nese history and Confucian culture, which communicated Chinese national identity to the public. By incorporating the shared Chinese regional and national history, typography and Confucian culture in relation to China's present and its past into the programs of these ceremonies, the National Games acted as an exemplary site for the presentation and representation of visible collective cultural and historical identity. In this respect, it had the capacity to imbue the Chinese people's sense of identity with unity, mean-ing and purpose so as to elevate the Chinese nation's prestige and image. The grand sports stadium itself and the media reports allowed thousands of spectators to experience the games either in person or at home. In watching the National Games, there was an increased opportunity for the develop-ment of common experiences and memories on the part of the imagined Chinese community. Hence, the National Games continued to be a national gathering to demonstrate national unity and national identity.

Additionally, in line with the reformation of China's sports policy to bal-ance the development between elite sport and mass sport, the National Games recently changed its public slogans to highlight that the National Games was not only a competition for the elite athletes but also a sports gala for the general public. This was clearly exemplified by the mottos of the 10th and 11th games: 'Sport's gala, people's festival' for the 10th National Games in 2005 and 'Harmonious China, people's games' for the 11th National Games in 2009. Moreover, there was an increased citizen's involvement in the pro-grammes of the games, including the ability to take part in the sport and cul-tural activities organized by the Organizing Committees or to be volunteers or audience members at the games.

Thus, it is concluded that this period in the history of the National Games in China (1983–2009) could be regarded as a stage of transformation. In the context of the globalization of sport, the National Games has experienced an Olympic-driven reformation since the 1980s. There is no doubt that the

Chinese government has continuously placed a high premium on the impact of the National Games on account of the part that it plays in the Olympic Strategy, which is to maintain the success of Chinese elite sport as a symbol of China's prestige and power in the world. In short, the longitudinal analysis of the nearly hundred-year history of the National Games in China (1910–2009) undertaken by this research project indicates that the National Games has continuously changed and developed to fulfil varying roles as was required at the time. It argues that the National Games has not been merely a sports gathering in China, but rather that it has reflected and been shaped by the differing situations, or contexts, of Chinese state-led nationalism in the modern and contemporary eras.

The hosting of mega-sports events has many positive effects on the hosting nations, or regions, across many aspects of society, including the economic, social, political and cultural dimensions and, particularly, on the project of obtaining political and cultural unity in the process of nation-building.[9] This book provides an insight into the evolution of the National Games as well as the dynamic interrelationship between the National Games and Chinese nationalism in the period from 1910 to 2009. It argues that the development of the National Games was shaped by Chinese nationalism as well as reflected the changing context of Chinese state-led nationalism in the modern and contemporary era. The overall structure of this book has been arranged to develop and provide evidence to support this argument.

The socio-historical analysis of the governance, operating system and dissemination of the National Games indicated that the National Games was not merely a sports event but also a catalyst for the nurturing of nationalist sentiment and national identity, which in turn bolstered the legitimacy of the ruling party. This research project illuminates the nature of the development and shifting governance structures of the National Games in response to broader national and international issues. It also reveals how these changes reflected the changing of the context of nationalism in China during these three distinct historical eras. Firstly, during the period from 1910 to 1948, the Third National Games in 1924 was used as a means to reclaim sports sovereignty from foreign ownership in China. This was part of a broader project of strengthening Chinese national autonomy and self-determination as an independent nation-state. In the 1930s and 1940s, under the Nanjing nationalist government the National Games, as a homegrown mega-sports event, assisted in the development of a sense of national identity in the modern Chinese nation-state. Secondly, from 1949 to 1979, the National Games was restored as a program for the national celebration of the new PRC. The National Games became a state-led sports event, which was guided and financially supported by the Chinese government. It had an intimate association with Chinese politics and was utilized to strengthen national defence, solidarity and cohesion, as well as to demonstrate the legitimacy of the CCP's authority. Thirdly, in the context of the globalization of sport, the development and reformation of the National Games from 1980 to 2009 was shaped by a more pragmatic form of Chinese nationalism in pursuit of economic modernization and national revival. The reformation of the National Games was Olympic-driven; it was utilized by the Chinese government to serve China's Olympic Strategy to achieve Olympic success. By serving China's Olympic Strategy, it assisted in the development of China's international prestige as well as national pride and morale. At the same time, the National Games adopted an IOC model of marketization and commercialization of sports events in order to run and support the National Games. This led to a gradual decentralization and commercialization of the National Games, in the process of which the games partly realized its own financial independence. Additionally, the performance of Chinese traditional culture at the ceremonies of the recent games stimulated national pride and functioned as a common memory underpinning national identity. It also communicated to its audience that the Chinese government, led by the CCP, had been, and would continue to be, the most significant defender of China's national political and economic interests.

The Western notion of nationalism was introduced to China more than a hundred years ago, and it has influenced China in various ways in the context of different political regimes. However, the consistent aim has remained the return of China to national greatness and the building of a sovereign nation-state. The spotlight on the National Games uncovers the reasons why sport in China has been so close to politics and how sport has contributed to the Chinese nation-building project of political and cultural integration and cohesion. This book is only a beginning to the critical examination of the relationship between national mega-sports events and politics in China, using the National Games as a case study. The complexity of this issue requires further research.

Notes

1 Morris, *Marrow of the Nation*, 9.
2 Sun, 'The Solution of China's Issue', 56.
3 Morris, *Marrow of the Nation*, 78.
4 Zhao, *A Nation-State by Construction*, 27–28.
5 Zhao, 'China's Pragmatic Nationalism', 131–144.
6 Zhao, 'Chinese Nationalism and Its International Orientations', 10.
7 Xu, *Olympic Dreams*, 197–198.
8 From interview material in China.
9 John Horne and Manzenreiter Wolfram, 'Sports Mega-Events: Social Scientific Analyses of a Global Phenomenon', *Sociological Review* 54, no. Suppl. 2 (2006): 1–187; Xu, 'Modernizing China in the Olympic Spotlight', 90–107.

References

Morris, Andrew D. *Marrow of the Nation: A History of Sport and Physical Culture in Republican China*. Berkeley and Los Angeles: University of California Press, 2004.

Sun, Yat-sen. 'The Solution of China's Issue.' In *The Selected Works of Sun Yat – sen*, edited by the Chinese Academy of Social Science, 53–68. Beijing: People's Press, 1956.

Xu, Guoqi. *Olympic Dreams: China and Sports, 1895–2008*. Cambridge, MA: Harvard University Press, 2009.

Xu, Xin. 'Modernizing China in the Olympic Spotlight: China's National Identity and the 2008 Beijing Olympiad.' *The Sociological Review* 54, no. 2 (2006): 90–107.

Zhao, Suisheng. 'China's Pragmatic Nationalism: Is It Manageable?' *The Washington Quarterly* 29, no. 1 (2005): 131–144.

Zhao, Suisheng. *A Nation-State by Construction: Dynamics of Modern Chinese Nationalism*. Stanford: Stanford University Press, 2004.

Zhao, Suisheng. 'Chinese Nationalism and Its International Orientations.' *Political Science Quarterly* 115, no. 1 (2000): 1–33.

Appendices

Appendix 1 The National Games in the late Qing Dynasty and the Republican China, 1910–1948

Year (Edition)	Host city	Competition program	Competition delegations	Athletes
1910 (First)	Nanjing	4	5	140
1914 (Second)	Wuchang	6	4	96
1924 (Third)	Beijing	7	4	340
1930 (Fourth)	Hangzhou	12	22	1,627
1933 (Fifth)	Nanjing	17	30	2,248
1935 (Sixth)	Shanghai	17	38	2,286
1948 (Seventh)	Shanghai	18	58	2,677

Source: 'The General Introduction of the National Games and the Medal-ranking', *The official website of the GASC*, Last modified on July 24, 2014, www.sport.gov.cn/n16/n1122/n1983/n32333/159582.html.

Appendix 2 The National Games in the PRC, 1959–2017

Year (Edition)	Host city	Competition program	Competition delegations	Athletes	Top three medals
1959 (First)	Beijing	29	36	7,707	PLA Beijing Shanghai
1965 (Second)	Beijing	30	22	5,922	PLA Shanghai Beijing
1975 (Third)	Beijing	31	28	7,302	Guangdong Beijing Shanghai
1979 (Fourth)	Beijing	31	34	3,824	PLA Beijing Guangdong
1983 (Fifth)	Shanghai	25	31	8,943	Guangdong, Shanghai Liaoning
1987 (Sixth)	Guangzhou	44	37	7,500	Guangdong Liaoning Shanghai
1993 (Seventh)	Beijing	43	45	8,000	Liaoning Guangdong Shanghai
1997 (Eighth)	Shanghai	28	46	7,647	Shanghai Liaoning Shandong
2001 (Ninth)	Guangzhou	30	45	8,608	Guangdong Liaoning PLA
2005 (10th)	Nanjing	32	46	9,986	Jiangsu Guangdong/PLA Shanghai
2009 (11th)	Jinan	33	46	11,183	Shandong PLA Jiangsu
2013 (12th)	Shenyang	31	38	9,770	Shandong Liaoning Guangdong
2017 (13th)	Tianjin	–	–	–	–

Source: 'The General Introduction of the National Games and the Medal-ranking', *The official website of the GASC*, Last modified on July 24, 2014, www.sport.gov.cn/n16/n1122/n1983/n32333/159582.html.

Index

Note: Page numbers in *italics* denote references to figures and tables.

self-governance of 108; sports
products companies donating to 44;
women's events 32
National Games Strategy 93
nationalism: categories of 3–5; holistic
view of 4–5; in name of patriotism 6;
sport and 7
Nationalist Party 4–5
National Products Movement 41–4,
108–9
national symbols: interaction rituals
and 12; visual impact of 97
nation-building: contribution of sports
to 9, 33, 115; definition of 1; history
of 2–3; mass media and 38; national
unity during process of 7; political
utility of sport in 109–10; purpose
of 1; sports goods companies and 44
nativist nationalism 51
new media 95, 103n52

Olympic Glory Plan 84
Olympic strategy 84, 85, 115
opening ceremonies: delegations'
parade at 66–7, *68*; Foucault on
66–7; guard of honour 67; Mao
Zedong attending 65–6; mass
calisthenics at 67–70, *69*; of Olympic
Games 90; politicization at 40, 65–6;
reception of Taiwanese delegation
60–1; of Sixth National Games 40;
state leaders attending *65*
'Open up the future' mass calisthenics
act 70
Opium War 3, 4

Patriotic Education Campaign 6
People's Daily 70–1, 73
People's Liberation Army (PLA) 58–9
People's Republic of China (PRC):
Beijing Worker's Stadium as symbol
of 58; founding of 2; sports policy
and governance 51–4; *see also*
China; National Games, in the PRC
physical education, importance of 26
Ping-Pong Diplomacy 53, 75
pomelos 61
posters, Third National Games *64*
pragmatic nationalism 5–6, 99
Provincial Sport Commission 58

Qing Dynasty: birth of National Games
73–4; birth of National Games in
28–9; fall of 4, 26–7; nation-building
from 2–3; support for study overseas
26; Western sport, introduction in
24, 107
Qingyi Bao (newspaper) 45n15

reformed competitive sports 87–8
rituals: definition of 11; of the Games
35–7, 107–8; interaction 10–12;
symbolic 35; visual impact of 97
Roberts, Kenneth 96
Roche, Maurice 31
Rogge, Jacques 90–1

Samaranch, Juan Antonio 90
satellite TV 97–8
Second National Games: in the PRC
55–6; of Republican era 29–30
Seoul Olympics 85
Seventh National Games: of the PRC
86, 89–90; of Republican era 34, 37
Shanghai Young Men's Christian
Association (YMCA) 23
Shao Yuanchong 36
Shi Ruisheng 39
Shi Xinglong 39
Shi Xinglu 39
Shi Xingwu 39
Singapore 9
Sino-Japanese War 34
Sixth National Games of Republican
era 34
Smith, Anthony D. 9
Socialism with Chinese Characteristics 83
socialist market economy 83
social media 98, 104n68
Soong Mei-ling 35
Spalding (sports goods company) 43
sport: competitive 12; contribution
to nation-building 9; as form of
interaction ritual 10–12; mass sport
52–4, 84–5, 95, 113; militarism
linked with 58–9; in missionary
schools 25; national identity and
7–10; nation-state's use of 11; as
political tool 13; as a ritual 12;
see also elite sports; Western sport
sports commercialization 83, 92, 111

For Product Safety Concerns and Information please contact our
EU representative GPSR@taylorandfrancis.com Taylor & Francis
Verlag GmbH, Kaufingerstraße 24, 80331 München, Germany